AF291719

THE DIVINE LITURGY

for

CHOIR AND LAITY

Published with the Blessing
of His Eminence Archbishop Laurus
of Syracuse and Holy Trinity Monastery

The Divine Liturgy for Choir and Laity
© 1992 Holy Trinity Monastery

ISBN: 978-0-88465-118-5

Second Printing, with revisions, 1998
Third Printing 2023

CONTENTS

INTRODUCTORY NOTE

This Divine Liturgy book is the successor to the typewritten editions of 1979, 1984, and 1986. It is designed to contain under one cover as much material as is necessary for the performing of the Divine Liturgy on all Sundays and major feast days. In addition, in the Menaion section are included saints of particular interest to people accustomed to the usage of the Russian Church Abroad. The text of the Liturgy conforms to the current usage of the Russian Church Abroad. All verses and quotations from the Psalms are according to the Psalter published by the Holy Transfiguration Monastery, Brookline, Mass. However, a word or two has been changed in certain psalm verses to agree with the Slavonic. Most of the Troparia and Kontakia are likewise largely according to manuscript translations of Holy Transfiguration Monastery which have been in circulation for twenty years or so. Many of the variable portions are based on various translations, but the final version is the work, i.e., the translation, revision, and/or choice of Rassaphor-monk Laurence, Holy Trinity Monastery, Jordanville, New York.

This is not an official text of the Russian Church Abroad.

The Procession of the Venerable Wood of the Cross, 1/14 August 1992

Second Printing, with revisions, Summer 1998

Priest: Blessed is our God, always, now and ever, and unto the ages of ages.

Reader: Amen. Glory to Thee, our God, glory to Thee.

O Heavenly King, Comforter, Spirit of truth, Who art everywhere present and fillest all things, Treasury of good things and Giver of life: Come and dwell in us, and cleanse us of all impurity, and save our souls, O Good One.

Holy God, Holy Mighty, Holy Immortal, have mercy on us. *Thrice.*

Glory to the Father, and to the Son, and to the Holy Spirit, both now and ever, and unto the ages of ages. Amen.

O Most Holy Trinity, have mercy on us. O Lord, blot out our sins. O Master, pardon our iniquities. O Holy One, visit and heal our infirmities for Thy name's sake.

Lord, have mercy. *Thrice.*

Glory to the Father, and to the Son, and to the Holy Spirit, both now and ever, and unto the ages of ages. Amen.

Our Father, Who art in the heavens, hallowed be Thy name. Thy kingdom come, Thy will be done, on earth as it is in heaven. Give us this day our daily bread, and forgive us our debts, as we forgive our debtors; and lead us not into temptation, but deliver us from the evil one.

Priest: For Thine is the kingdom and the power, and the glory: of the Father and of the Son, and of the Holy Spirit, now and ever, and unto the ages of ages.

Reader: Amen. Lord, have mercy. *Twelve.*

Glory to the Father, and to the Son, and to the Holy Spirit, both now and ever, and unto the ages of ages. Amen.

O come, let us worship God our King.

O come, let us worship and fall down before Christ our King and God.

O come, let us worship and fall down before Christ Himself, our King and God.

PSALM 16

Hearken, O Lord, unto my righteousness, attend unto my supplication. Give ear unto my prayer, which cometh not from deceitful lips. From before Thy face let my judgment come forth, let mine eyes behold uprightness. Thou hast proved my heart, Thou hast visited it in the night, Thou hast tried me by fire, and unrighteousness was not found in me. That my mouth might not speak of the works of men, for the sake of the words of Thy lips have I kept the ways that are hard. Set my footsteps in Thy paths, that my steps may not be shaken. I have cried, for Thou hast hearkened unto me, O God. Incline Thine ear unto me, and hearken unto my words. Let Thy mercies be made wonderful, O Thou that savest them that hope in Thee. From them that have resisted Thy right hand, keep me, O Lord, as the apple of Thine eye. In the shelter of Thy wings wilt Thou shelter me, from the face of the ungodly which have oppressed me. Mine enemies have surround-ed my soul, they have enclosed themselves with their own fat, their mouth hath spoken pride. They that cast me out have now encir-cled me, they have set their eyes to look askance on the earth. They have taken me as might a lion ready for his prey, and as might a lion's whelp that dwelleth in hiding. Arise, O

Lord, overtake them and trip their heels; deliver my soul from ungodly men, Thy sword from the enemies of Thy hand. O Lord, from Thy few do Thou separate them from the earth in their life; yea, with Thy hidden treasures hath their belly been filled. They have satisfied themselves with swine and have left the remnants to their babes. But as for me, in righteousness shall I appear before Thy face; I shall be filled when Thy glory is made manifest to me.

PSALM 24

Unto Thee, O Lord, have I lifted up my soul. O my God, in Thee have I trusted; let me never be put to shame, nor let mine enemies laugh me to scorn. Yea, let none that wait on Thee be put to shame; let them be ashamed which are lawless without a cause. Make Thy ways, O Lord, known unto me and teach me Thy paths. Lead me in Thy truth and teach me, for Thou art God my Saviour; for on Thee have I waited all the day long. Remember Thy compassions, O Lord, and Thy mercies, for they are from everlasting. The sins of my youth and mine ignorances remember not; according to Thy mercy remember Thou me, for the sake of Thy goodness, O Lord. Good and upright is the Lord; therefore will He set a law for them that sin in the way. He will guide the meek in judgment, He will teach the meek His ways. All the ways of the Lord are mercy and truth, unto them that seek after His covenant and His testimonies. For the sake of Thy name, O Lord, be gracious unto my sin; for it is great. Who is the man that feareth the Lord? He will set him a law in the way which He hath chosen. His soul shall dwell among good things, and his seed shall inherit the earth. The Lord is the strength of them that fear Him, and His covenant shall be manifested unto them. Mine eyes are ever toward the Lord, for He it is that will draw my feet out of the snare. Look upon me, and have mercy on me; for I am one only-begotten and poor. The afflictions of my heart are multiplied; bring me out from my necessities. Behold my lowliness and my toil, and forgive all my sins. Look upon mine enemies, for they are multiplied, and with an unjust hatred have they hated me. Keep my soul and rescue me;

let me not be put to shame, for I have hoped in Thee. The innocent and the upright have cleaved unto me, for I waited on Thee, O Lord. Redeem Israel, O God, out of all his afflictions.

PSALM 50

Have mercy on me, O God, according to Thy great mercy; and according to the multitude of Thy compassions blot out my transgression. Wash me thoroughly from mine iniquity, and cleanse me from my sin. For I know mine inquity, and my sin is ever before me. Against Thee only have I sinned and done this evil before Thee, that Thou mightest be justified in Thy words, and prevail when Thou art judged. For behold, I was conceived in iniquities, and in sins did my mother bear me. For behold, Thou hast loved truth; the hidden and secret things of Thy wisdom hast Thou made manifest unto me. Thou shalt sprinkle me with hyssop, and I shall be made clean; Thou shalt wash me, and I shall be made whiter than snow. Thou shalt make me to hear joy and gladness; the bones that be humbled, they shall rejoice. Turn Thy face away from my sins, and blot out all mine iniquities. Create in me a clean heart, O God, and renew a right spirit within me. Cast me not away from Thy presence, and take not Thy Holy spirit from me. Restore unto me the joy of Thy salvation, and with Thy governing Spirit establish me. I shall teach transgressors Thy ways, and the ungodly shall turn back unto Thee. Deliver me from blood-guiltiness, O God, Thou God of my salvation; my tongue shall rejoice in Thy righteousness. O Lord, Thou shalt open my lips, and my mouth shall declare Thy praise. For if Thou hadst desired sacrifice, I had given it; with whole-burnt offerings Thou shalt not be pleased. A sacrifice unto God is a broken spirit; a heart that is broken and humbled God will not despise. Do good, O Lord, in Thy good pleasure unto Sion, and let the walls of Jerusalem be builded. Then shalt Thou be pleased with a sacrifice of righteousness, with oblation and whole-burnt offerings. Then shall they offer bullocks upon Thine altar.

Glory to the Father, and to the Son, and to the Holy Spirit, both now and ever, and unto

the ages of ages. Amen.

Alleluia, alleluia, alleluia. Glory to Thee, O God. *Thrice.*

Lord, have mercy. *Thrice.*

If there be two troparia, we say the first one here. (See pages 110-276 for troparia). If not, we continue:

Glory to the Father, and to the Son, and to the Holy Spirit. *And we say the second troparion, if any, or the only troparion. Then:*

Both now and ever, and unto the ages of ages. Amen.

Theotokion: O Theotokos, thou art the true vine that hath blossomed forth for us the Fruit of life. Thee do we supplicate: Intercede, O Lady, together with the holy apostles, that our souls find mercy.

Blessed is the Lord God, blessed is the Lord day by day; the God of our salvation shall prosper us along the way; our God is the God of salvation.

Holy God, Holy Mighty, Holy Immortal, have mercy on us. *Thrice.*

Glory to the Father, and to the Son, and to the Holy Spirit, both now and ever, and unto

the ages of ages. Amen.

O Most Holy Trinity, have mercy on us. O Lord, blot out our sins. O Master, pardon our iniquities. O Holy One, visit and heal our infirmities for Thy name's sake.

Lord, have mercy. *Thrice.*

Glory to the Father, and to the Son, and to the Holy Spirit, both now and ever, and unto the ages of ages. Amen.

Our Father, Who art in the heavens, hallowed be Thy name. Thy kingdom come, Thy will be done, on earth as it is in heaven. Give us this day our daily bread, and forgive us our debts, as we forgive our debtors; and lead us not into temptation, but deliver us from the evil one.

Priest: For Thine is the kingdom, and the power, and the glory: of the Father, and of the Son, and of the Holy Spirit, now and ever, and unto the ages of ages.

Reader: Amen. And we read the appointed kontakion. (See pages 110-276 for kontakia.) If there be two kontakia, we read the one that was chanted after the 6th Ode of the canons at Matins. Then:

Lord, have mercy. *Forty times. And the Prayer of the Hours:*

Thou Who at all times and at every hour, in heaven and on earth, art worshipped and glorified, O Christ God, Who art long-suffering, plenteous in mercy, most compassionate, Who lovest the righteous and hast mercy on sinners, Who callest all to salvation through the promise of good things to come: Receive, O Lord, our prayers at this hour, and guide our life toward Thy commandments. Sanctify our souls, make chaste our bodies, correct our thoughts, purify our intentions, and deliver us from every sorrow, evil, and pain. Compass us about with Thy holy angels, that, guarded and guided by their array, we may attain to the unity of the faith, and the knowledge of Thine unapproachable glory; for blessed art Thou unto the ages of ages. Amen.

Lord, have mercy. *Thrice.*

Glory to the Father, and to the Son, and to the Holy Spirit, both now and ever, and unto the ages of ages. Amen.

More honorable than the Cherubim, and beyond compare more glorious than the Seraphim, who without corruption gavest birth to God the Word, the very Theotokos, thee do we magnify.

In the name of the Lord, father (master), bless.

Priest: Through the prayers of our holy fathers, O Lord Jesus Christ our God, have mercy on us.

Reader: Amen. *Then the Prayer of St. Mardarius:*

O Master, God the Father Almighty, O Lord, the Only-begotten Son, Jesus Christ, and O Holy Spirit, one Godhead, one Power: Have mercy on me a sinner, and by the judgments which Thou knowest, save me, Thine unworthy servant; for blessed art Thou unto the ages of ages. Amen.

THE END OF THE THIRD HOUR

❄❄❄❄❄❄

O come, let us worship God our King.

O come, let us worship and fall down before Christ our King and God.

O come, let us worship and fall down before Christ Himself, our King and God.

PSALM 53

O God in Thy name save me, and in Thy strength do Thou judge me. O God, hearken unto my prayer, give ear unto the words of my mouth. For strangers are risen up against me, and mighty men have sought after my soul and have not set God before themselves. For behold, God helpeth me, and the Lord is the protector of my soul. He will bring evils upon mine enemies. Utterly destroy them by Thy truth. Willingly shall I sacrifice unto Thee; I will confess Thy name, O Lord, for it is good. For out of every affliction hast Thou delivered me, and mine eye hath looked down upon mine enemies.

PSALM 54

Give ear, O God, unto my prayer, and disdain not my supplication; attend unto me, and hear me. I was grieved in my meditation,

and I was troubled at the voice of the enemy
and the oppression of the sinner; Because they
have turned iniquity upon me, and with wrath
were they angry against me. My heart is troubled within me, and the terror of death is fall-
en upon me. Fear and trembling are come
upon me, and darkness hath covered me. And
I said: Who will give me wings like a dove?
And I will fly, and be at rest. Lo, I have fled
afar off and have dwelt in the wilderness. I
waited for God that saveth me from faint-
heartedness and from tempest. Plunge them
into the depths, O Lord, and divide their
tongues, for I have seen iniquity and gainsay-
ing in the city. Day and night they go round
about her upon her walls; iniquity and toil and
unrighteousness are in midst of her. And
usury and deceit have not departed from her
streets. For if mine enemy had reviled me, I
might have endured it. And if he that hateth
me had spoken boastful words against me, I
might have hid myself from him. But thou it
was, O man of like soul with me, my guide and
my familiar friend, thou who together with me
didst sweeten my repasts; in the house of God

I walked with thee in oneness of mind. Let death come upon such ones, and let them go down alive into hades. For wickedness is in their dwellings, and in the midst of them. As for me, unto God have I cried, and the Lord hearkened unto me. Evening, morning, and noonday will I tell of it and will declare it, and He will hear my voice. He will redeem my soul in peace from them that draw nigh unto me, for they among many were with me. God will hear, and He will humble them, He that is before the ages. For to them there is no requital, because they have not feared God; He hath stretched forth His hand in retribution. They have defiled His covenant; they were scattered by the wrath of His countenance, and their hearts have convened. Their words were smoother than oil, and yet they are darts. Cast thy care upon the Lord, and He will nourish thee; He will never permit the righteous to be shaken. But Thou, O God, shalt bring those men down into the pit of destruction. Bloody and deceitful men shall not live out half their days; but as for me, O Lord, I will hope in Thee.

PSALM 90

He that dwelleth in the help of the Most High shall abide in the shelter of the God of heaven. He shall say unto the Lord: Thou art my helper and my refuge. He is my God, and I will hope in Him. For He shall deliver thee from the snare of the hunters and from every troubling word. With His shoulders will He overshadow thee, and under His wings shalt thou have hope. With a shield will His truth encompass thee; thou shalt not be afraid for the terror by night, nor for the arrow that flieth by day, nor for the thing that walketh in darkness, nor for the mishap and demon of noonday. A thousand shall fall at thy side, and ten thousand at thy right hand, but unto thee shalt it not come nigh. Only with thine eyes shalt thou behold, and thou shalt see the reward of sinners. For Thou, O Lord, art my hope. Thou madest the Most High thy refuge; no evils shall come nigh thee, and no scourge shall draw nigh unto thy dwelling. For He shall give His angels charge over thee, to keep thee in all thy ways. On their hands shall they bear thee up, lest at any time thou dash thy foot against a stone. Upon the asp and basilisk shalt thou tread, and thou shalt trample upon the lion and dragon. For he hath set his hope on Me, and I will deliver him; I will shelter him because he hath known My name. He shall cry unto Me, and I will hearken unto him. I am with him in affliction, and I will rescue him and glorify him. With length of days will I satisfy him, and I will show him My salvation.

Glory to the Father, and to the Son, and to the Holy Spirit, both now and ever, and unto the ages of ages. Amen.

Alleluia, alleluia, alleluia. Glory to Thee, O God. *Thrice.*

Lord, have mercy. *Thrice. If there be two troparia, we say the first one here. (See pages 110-276 for troparia). If not, we continue:*

Glory to the Father, and to the Son, and to the Holy Spirit. *And we say the second troparion, if any, or the only troparion. Then:*

Both now and ever, and unto the ages of ages. Amen.

Theotokion: Seeing that we have no boldness on account of our many sins, do thou beseech Him that was born of thee, O Virgin

Theotokos; for the supplication of a mother availeth much to win the Master's favour. Disdain not the prayers of sinners, O all-pure one, for merciful and mighty to save is He, Who deigned also to suffer for our sake.

Let Thy compassions quickly go before us, O Lord, for we are become exceedingly poor. Help us, O God, our Saviour, for the sake of the glory of Thy name; O Lord, deliver us and be gracious unto our sins for Thy name's sake.

Holy God, Holy Mighty, Holy Immortal, have mercy on us. *Thrice.*

Glory to the Father, and to the Son, and to the Holy Spirit, both now and ever, and unto the ages of ages. Amen.

O Most Holy Trinity, have mercy on us. O Lord, blot out our sins. O Master, pardon our iniquities. O Holy One, visit and heal our infirmities for Thy name's sake.

Lord, have mercy. *Thrice.*

Glory to the Father, and to the Son, and to the Holy Spirit, both now and ever, and unto the ages of ages. Amen.

Our Father, Who art in the heavens, hallowed be Thy name. Thy kingdom come, Thy will be done, on earth as it is in heaven. Give us this day our daily bread, and forgive us our debts, as we forgive our debtors; and lead us not into temptation, but deliver us from the evil one.

Priest: For Thine is the kingdom, and the power, and the glory: of the Father, and of the Son, and of the Holy Spirit, now and ever, and unto the ages of ages.

Reader: Amen. *And we read the appointed kontakion. (See pages 110-276 for kontakia.) If there be two kontakia, we read the one that was chanted after the 3rd Ode of the canons at Matins. Then:*

Lord, have mercy. *Forty times. And the Prayer of the Hours:*

Thou Who at all times and at every hour, in heaven and on earth, art worshipped and glorified, O Christ God, Who art long-suffering, plenteous in mercy, most compassionate, Who lovest the righteous and hast mercy on sinners, Who callest all to salvation through the promise of good things to come: Receive, O Lord, our prayers at this hour, and guide our life toward Thy commandments. Sanctify our souls, make chaste our bodies, correct our thoughts, purify our intentions, and deliver us from every sorrow, evil, and pain. Compass us about with Thy holy angels, that, guarded and guided by their array, we may attain to the unity of the faith, and the knowledge of Thine unapproachable glory; for blessed art Thou unto the ages of ages. Amen.

Lord, have mercy. *Thrice.*

Glory to the Father, and to the Son, and to the Holy Spirit, both now and ever, and unto the ages of ages. Amen.

More honorable than the Cherubim, and beyond compare more glorious than the Seraphim, who without corruption gavest birth to God the Word, the very Theotokos, thee do we magnify.

In the name of the Lord, father (master), bless.

Priest: Through the prayers of our holy fathers, O Lord Jesus Christ our God, have mercy on us.

Reader: Amen. *Then the Prayer of Basil the Great:*

O God and Lord of Hosts, and Maker of all creation, Who by the tender compassion of Thy mercy which transcendeth comprehension, didst send down Thine Only-begotten Son, our Lord Jesus Christ, for the salvation of our race, and by His precious Cross didst tear asunder the handwriting of our sins, and thereby didst triumph over the principalites and powers of darkness: Do Thou Thyself, O Master, Lover of mankind, accept also from us sinners these prayers of thanksgiving and entreaty, and deliver us from every destructive and dark transgression, and from all enemies, both visible and invisible, that seek to do us evil. Nail down our flesh with the fear of Thee, and incline not our hearts unto words or thoughts of evil, but pierce our souls with longing for Thee, so that ever looking to Thee, and being guided by Thy light as we behold Thee, the unapproachable and everlasting Light, we may send up unceasing praise and thanksgiving unto Thee, the unoriginate Father, with Thine Only-begotten Son, and Thine All-holy and good and life-creating Spirit, now and ever, and unto the ages of ages. Amen.

THE END OF THE SIXTH HOUR

THE ORDER OF PREPARATION FOR HOLY COMMUNION

Through the prayers of our holy fathers, O Lord Jesus Christ our God, have mercy on us. Amen.

Glory to Thee, our God, glory to Thee.

O Heavenly King, Comforter, Spirit of Truth, Who art everywhere present and fillest all things, Treasury of good things and Giver of life: Come and dwell in us, and cleanse us of all impurity, and save our souls, O Good One.

Holy God, Holy Mighty, Holy Immortal, have mercy on us. *Thrice.*

Glory to the Father, and to the Son, and to the Holy Spirit, both now and ever, and unto the ages of ages. Amen.

O Most Holy Trinity, have mercy on us. O Lord, blot out our sins. O Master, pardon our iniquities. O Holy One, visit and heal our infirmities for Thy name's sake.

Lord, have mercy. *Thrice.*

Glory to the Father, and to the Son, and to the Holy Spirit, both now and ever, and unto the ages of ages. Amen.

Our Father, Who art in the heavens, hallowed be Thy name. Thy kingdom come, Thy will be done, on earth as it is in heaven. Give us this day our daily bread, and forgive us our debts, as we forgive our debtors; and lead us not into temptation, but deliver us from the evil one.

Lord, have mercy. *Twelve times.*

Glory to the Father, and to the Son, and to the Holy Spirit, both now and ever, and unto the ages of ages. Amen.

O come, let us worship God our King.

O come, let us worship and fall down before Christ our King and God.

O come, let us worship and fall down before Christ Himself, our King and God.

PSALM 22

The Lord is my shepherd, and I shall not want. In a place of green pasture, there hath He made me to dwell; beside the water of rest hath He nurtured me. He hath converted my soul, He hath led me on the paths of righteousness for His name's sake. For though I should walk in the midst of the shadow of death, I will fear no evil, for Thou art with me;

Thy rod and Thy staff, they have comforted me. Thou hast prepared a table before me in the presence of them that afflict me. Thou hast anointed my head with oil, and Thy cup which filleth me, how excellent it is! And Thy mercy shall pursue me all the days of my life, and I will dwell in the house of the Lord unto length of days.

PSALM 23

The earth is the Lord's and the fullness thereof, the world, and all that dwell therein. He hath founded it upon the seas, and upon the rivers hath He prepared it. Who shall ascend into the mountain of the Lord? Or who shall stand in His holy place? He that is innocent in hands, and pure in heart, who hath not received his soul in vain, and hath not sworn deceitfully to his neighbour. Such a one shall receive a blessing from the Lord, and mercy from God his Saviour. This is the generation of them that seek the Lord, of them that seek the face of the God of Jacob. Lift up your gates, O ye princes; and be ye lifted up, ye everlasting gates, and the King of Glory shall enter in. Who is this King of Glory? The

Lord strong and mighty, the Lord, mighty in war. Lift up your gates, O ye princes; and be ye lifted up, ye everlasting gates, and the King of Glory shall enter in. Who is this King of Glory? The Lord of hosts, He is the King of Glory.

PSALM 115

I believed, wherefore I spake; I was humbled exceedingly. As for me, I said in mine ecstasy: Every man is a liar. What shall I render unto the Lord for all that He hath rendered unto me? I will take the cup of salvation, and I will call upon the name of the Lord. My vows unto the Lord will I pay in the presence of all His people. Precious in the sight of the Lord is the death of His saints. O Lord, I am Thy servant; I am Thy servant and the son of Thy handmaid. Thou hast broken my bonds asunder. I will sacrifice a sacrifice of praise unto Thee, and I will call upon the name of the Lord. My vows unto the Lord will I pay in the presence of all His people, in the courts of the house of the Lord, in the midst of thee, O Jerusalem.

Glory to the Father, and to the Son, and to the Holy Spirit, both now and ever, and unto

the ages of ages. Amen.

Alleluia, alleluia, alleluia. Glory to Thee, O God. *Thrice.*

Lord, have mercy. *Thrice.*

Troparia, Eighth Tone:

Disregard my transgressions, O Lord Who wast born of a Virgin, and purify my heart, and make it a temple for Thy spotless Body and Blood. Let me not be rejected from Thy presence, O Thou Who hast great mercy without measure.

Glory to the Father, and to the Son, and to the Holy Spirit.

How can I who am unworthy dare to come to the Communion of Thy Holy Things? For if I should dare to approach Thee with those that are worthy, my garment betrayeth me, for it is not a festal robe, and I shall cause the condemnation of my greatly-sinful soul. Cleanse, O Lord, the pollution from my soul, and save me, as Thou art the Lover of mankind.

Both now and ever, and unto the ages of ages. Amen.

Greatly multiplied, O Theotokos, are my sins; unto thee have I fled, O pure one, im-

ploring salvation. Do thou visit mine enfee-
bled soul, and pray to thy Son and our God
that He grant me forgiveness for the evil I have
done, O thou only blessed one.

During Holy and Great Lent say this:

When the glorious disciples were enlightened at the washing of the feet, then Judas the
ungodly one was stricken and darkened with
the love of silver. And unto the lawless judges
did he deliver Thee, the righteous Judge.
Behold, O lover of money, him that for the
sake thereof did hang himself; flee from that
insatiable soul that dared such things against
the Master. Thou Who art good unto all, O
Lord, glory be to Thee.

PSALM 50

Have mercy on me, O God, according to
Thy great mercy; and according to the
multitude of Thy compassions blot out my
transgression. Wash me thoroughly from
mine iniquity, and cleanse me from my sin.
For I know mine iniquity, and my sin is ever
before me. Against Thee only have I sinned
and done this evil before Thee, that Thou
mightest be justified in Thy words, and prevail

when Thou art judged. For behold, I was conceived in iniquities, and in sins did my mother bear me. For behold, Thou hast loved truth; the hidden and secret things of Thy wisdom hast Thou made manifest unto me. Thou shalt sprinkle me with hyssop, and I shall be made clean; Thou shalt wash me, and I shall be made whiter than snow. Thou shalt make me to hear joy and gladness; the bones that be humbled, they shall rejoice. Turn Thy face away from my sins, and blot out all mine iniquities. Create in me a clean heart, O God, and renew a right spirit within me. Cast me not away from Thy presence, and take not Thy Holy Spirit from me. Restore unto me the joy of Thy salvation, and with Thy governing Spirit establish me, I shall teach transgressors Thy ways, and the ungodly shall turn back unto Thee. Deliver me from blood-guiltiness, O God, Thou God of my salvation; my tongue shall rejoice in Thy righteousness. O Lord, Thou shalt open my lips, and my mouth shall declare Thy praise. For if Thou hadst desired sacrifice, I had given it; with whole-burnt offerings Thou shalt not be pleased. A sacrifice unto God is broken spirit; a heart that is broken and humbled God will not despise. Do good, O Lord, in Thy good pleasure unto Sion, and let the walls of Jerusalem be builded. Then shalt Thou be pleased with a sacrifice of righteousness, with oblation and whole-burnt offerings. Then shall they offer bullocks upon Thine altar.

And immediately the Canon, Second Tone:

ODE I

Eirmos: Come, O ye people, let us sing a hymn to Christ our God, Who divided the sea and guided the people whom He brought out of the bondage of Egypt, for He is glorified.

Refrain: Create in me a clean heart, O God, and renew a right spirit within me.

May Thy holy Body be unto me the Bread of life eternal, O Compassionate Lord, and Thy precious Blood be also the healing of many forms of illness.

Refrain: Cast me not away from Thy presence, and take not Thy Holy Spirit from me.

Defiled by unseemly deeds, I the wretched one am unworthy, O Christ, of the communion of Thy most pure Body and divine Blood, which do Thou vouchsafe me.

Glory to the Father, and to the Son, and to the Holy Spirit, both now and ever, and unto the ages of ages. Amen.

O blessed Bride of God, O good soil that grew the Corn untilled and saving to the world, vouchsafe me to be saved by eating It.

ODE III

Eirmos: By establishing me on the rock of faith, Thou hast enlarged my mouth over mine enemies, for my spirit rejoiceth when I sing: There is none holy as our God, and none righteous beside Thee, O Lord.

Refrain: Create in me a clean heart, O God, and renew a right spirit within me.

Teardrops grant me, O Christ, to cleanse my defiled heart, that, purified and with a good conscience, I may come with faith and fear, O Master, to the communion of Thy divine Gifts.

Refrain: Cast me not away from Thy presence, and take not Thy Holy Spirit from me.

May Thy most pure Body and divine Blood be unto me for remission of sins, for communion with the Holy Spirit, and unto life eternal, O Lover of mankind, and to the estrangement of passions and sorrows.

Glory to the Father, and to the Son, and to the Holy Spirit, both now and ever, and unto the ages of ages. Amen.

O thou Most Holy table of the Bread of Life that for mercy's sake came down from on high, giving new life to the world, vouchsafe even me, the unworthy, to eat it with fear, and live.

ODE IV

Eirmos: From a Virgin didst Thou come, not as an ambassador nor as an angel, but the very Lord Himself incarnate and didst save me, the whole man. Wherefore, I cry to Thee: Glory to Thy power, O Lord.

Refrain: Create in me a clean heart, O God, and renew a right spirit within me.

O Thou Who wast incarnate for our sake, O Most-merciful One, Thou didst will to be slain as a sheep for the sin mankind. Wherefore, I entreat Thee to blot out my sins also.

Refrain: Cast me not away from Thy presence, and take not Thy Holy Spirit from me.

Heal the wounds of my soul, O Lord, and sanctify all of me, and vouchsafe, O Master, that I, the wretched one, may partake of Thy divine Mystical Supper.

Glory to the Father, and to the Son, and to the Holy Spirit, both now and ever, and unto the ages of ages. Amen.

Propitiate for me also Him that came from thy womb, O Lady, and keep me, thy servant, undefiled and blameless, so that by obtaining the spiritual Pearl I may be sanctified.

ODE V

Eirmos: O Lord, Giver of light and Creator of the ages, guide us in the light of Thy commandments, for we know none other God beside Thee.

Refrain: Create in me a clean heart, O God, and renew a right spirit within me.

As Thou didst foretell, O Christ, so let it be unto Thy wicked servant, and in me abide, as Thou didst promise; for behold, I eat Thy divine Body and drink Thy Blood.

Refrain: Cast me not away from Thy presence, and take not Thy Holy Spirit from me.

O Word of God and God, may the live coal of Thy Body be unto the enlightenment of me who am in darkness, and Thy Blood unto the cleansing of my defiled soul.

Glory to the Father, and to the Son, and to the Holy Spirit, both now and ever, and unto the ages of ages. Amen.

O Mary, Mother of God, precious tabernacle of fragrance, through thy prayers make me a chosen vessel, that I may partake of the Sacrament of thy Son.

ODE VI

Eirmos: Whirled about in the abyss of sin, I

appeal to the unfathomable abyss of Thy compassion: From corruption raise me up, O God.

Refrain: Create in me a clean heart, O God, and renew a right spirit within me.

O Saviour, sanctify my mind, my soul, my heart, and my body, and vouchsafe me uncondemned, O Master, to approach the fearful Mysteries.

Refrain: Cast me not away from Thy presence, and take not Thy Holy Spirit from me.

Grant that I may be rid of passions, and have the assistance of Thy grace, and strengthening of life by the communion of Thy holy Mysteries, O Christ.

Glory to the Father, and to the Son, and to the Holy Spirit, both now and ever, and unto the ages of ages. Amen.

O Holy Word of God and God, sanctify all of me as I now come to Thy divine Mysteries, through the prayers of Thy holy Mother.

Lord, have mercy. *Thrice*

Glory to the Father, and to the Son, and to the Holy Spirit, both now and ever, and unto the ages of ages. Amen.

Kontakion, Second Tone:

Count me not unworthy, O Christ, to receive now the Bread which is Thy Body, and

Thy Divine Blood, and to partake, O Master, of Thy most pure and dread Mysteries, wretched though I be. Let these not be for me unto judgment, but unto life immortal and everlasting.

ODE VII

Eirmos: The wise children did not serve the golden image, but went themselves into the flame and reviled the pagan gods. They cried in the midst of the flame, and the angel bedewed them: Already the prayer of your lips was heard.

Refrain: Create in me a clean heart, O God, and renew a right spirit within me.

May the communion of Thine immortal Mysteries, the source of blessings, O Christ, be to me now light, and life, and dispassion, and for progress and increase in the most divine virtues, O only Good One, that I may glorify Thee.

Refrain: Cast me not away from Thy presence, and take not Thy Holy Spirit from me.

That I may be delivered from passions, and enemies, need, and every sorrow, I now draw nigh with trembling, love, and reverence, O Lover of mankind, to Thine immortal and divine Mysteries. Vouchsafe me to hymn Thee: Blessed art Thou, O Lord God of our fathers.

Glory to the Father, and to the Son, and to the Holy Spirit, both now and ever, and unto the ages of ages. Amen.

O thou who art full of grace, who beyond understanding gavest birth to Christ the Saviour, I thy servant, the impure, now entreat thee, the pure: Cleanse me, who am now about to approach the most pure Mysteries, from all defilement of flesh and spirit.

ODE VIII

Eirmos: God Who descended into the fiery furnace unto the Hebrew children and changed the flame into dew, praise Him as Lord, O ye works, and supremely exalt Him unto all the ages.

Refrain: Create in me a clean heart, O God, and renew a right spirit within me.

Of Thy heavenly and dread holy Mysteries, O Christ, and of Thy divine Mystical Supper vouchsafe now even me, the despairing one, to partake, O God my Saviour.

Refrain: Cast me not away from Thy presence, and take not Thy Holy Spirit from me.

Fleeing for refuge to Thy loving-kindness, O Good One, with fear I cry unto Thee: Abide in me, O Saviour, and I, as Thou hast said, in Thee. For behold, presuming on Thy mercy, I eat Thy Body and drink Thy Blood.

Glory to the Father, and to the Son, and to the Holy Spirit, both now and ever, and unto the ages of ages. Amen.

I tremble at taking fire, lest I be consumed as wax and grass. O fearful Mystery! O the loving-kindness of God! How is it that I, being but clay, partake of the divine Body and Blood, and am made incorruptible?

ODE IX

Eirmos: The Son of the unoriginate Father, God and Lord, hath appeared unto us incarnate of the Virgin, to enlighten those in darkness and to gather the dispersed. Wherefore, the all-hymned Theotokos do we magnify.

Refrain: Create in me a clean heart, O God, and renew a right spirit within me.

Christ It is, O taste and see! The Lord for our sake made like unto us of old, once offered Himself as an offering to His Father, and is ever slain, sanctifying them that partake.

Refrain: Cast me not away from Thy presence, and take not Thy Holy Spirit from me.

May I be sanctified in soul and body, O Master, may I be enlightened, may I be saved, may I become Thy dwelling through the communion of Thy holy Mysteries, having Thee with the Father and the Spirit living in me, O Benefactor plenteous in mercy.

Glory to the Father, and to the Son, and to the Holy Spirit.

May Thy Body and Thy most precious Blood, O my Saviour, be unto me as fire and light, consuming the substance of sin, and burning the thorns of passions, and enlightening all of me to worship Thy Divinity.

Both now and ever, and unto the ages of ages. Amen.

God took flesh of thy pure blood; wherefore, all generations do hymn thee, O Lady, and throngs of heavenly minds glorify thee, for through thee they have clearly seen Him Who ruleth all things endued with human nature.

And immediately: It is truly meet to bless thee, the Theotokos, ever-blessed and most blameless, and Mother of our God. More honourable than the Cherubim, and beyond compare more glorious than the Seraphim, who without corruption gavest birth to God the Word, the very Theotokos, thee do we magnify.

Holy God, Holy Mighty, Holy Immortal,

have mercy on us. *Thrice.*

Glory to the Father, and to the Son, and to the Holy Spirit, both now and ever, and unto the ages of ages. Amen.

O Most Holy Trinity, have mercy on us. O Lord, blot out our sins. O Master, pardon our iniquities. O Holy One, visit and heal our infirmities for Thy name's sake.

Lord, have mercy. *Thrice.*

Glory to the Father, and to the Son, and to the Holy Spirit, both now and ever, and unto the ages of ages. Amen.

Our Father, Who art in the heavens, hallowed be Thy name. Thy kingdom come, Thy will be done, on earth as it is in heaven. Give us this day our daily bread, and forgive us our debts, as we forgive our debtors; and lead us not into temptation, but deliver us from the evil one.

Then the troparion of the day, if it be the feast of Christ's Nativity, or another feast of the Lord. If it be Sunday, the troparion of the resurrection of the tone. If not, these:

Sixth Tone:

Have mercy on us, O Lord, have mercy on

us; for at a loss for any defence, this prayer do we sinners offer unto Thee as Master: have mercy on us.

Glory to the Father, and to the Son, and to the Holy Spirit.

Lord, have mercy on us, for we have hoped in Thee, be not angry with us greatly, neither remember our iniquities; but look upon us now as Thou art compassionate, and deliver us from our enemies, for Thou art our God, and we, Thy people; all are the works of Thy hands, and we call upon Thy name.

Both now and ever, and unto the ages of ages. Amen.

Theotokion: The door of compassion open unto us, O blessed Theotokos, for, hoping in thee, let us not perish; through thee may we be delivered from adversities, for thou art the salvation of the Christian race.

Then: Lord, have mercy. *Forty times. And reverences (bows or prostrations), as many as thou desirest.*

And thereafter, these lines:

If thou desirest, O man, to eat the Body of the Master,

Approach with fear, lest thou be burnt; for It is fire.

And when thou drinkest the Divine Blood unto communion,

First be reconciled to them that have griev-ed thee,

Then dare to eat the Mystical Food.

Other lines:

Before partaking of the awesome Sacrifice
Of the life-giving Body of the Master,
After this manner pray with trembling.

A Prayer of Basil the Great, 1:

O Master Lord Jesus Christ our God, Source of life and immortality, Creator of all things visible and invisible, the co-eternal and co-unoriginate Son of the unoriginate Father, Who, out of Thy great goodness, didst in the latter days clothe Thyself in flesh, and wast crucified, and buried for us ungrateful and evil-disposed ones, and hast renewed with Thine Own Blood our nature corrupted by sin: Do Thou Thyself, O Immortal King, accept the repentance of me a sinner, and incline Thine ear to me, and hearken unto my words. For I have sinned against heaven and before Thee, and I am not worthy to look upon the height of Thy glory; for I have angered Thy goodness by transgressing Thy commandments and not obeying Thine injunctions. But Thou, O Lord, Who art not vengeful, but long-suffering and plenteous in mercy, hast not given me over to be destroyed with my sins, but always Thou awaitest my complete conversion. For Thou hast said, O Lover of mankind, through Thy prophet: For I desire not the death of the sinner, but that he should return and live. For Thou desirest not, O Master, to destroy the work of Thy hands, neither shalt Thou be pleased with the destruction of men, but desirest that all be saved and come to a knowledge of the truth. Wherefore, even I, although unworthy of heaven and earth, and of this temporal life, having submitted my whole self to sin, and made myself a slave of pleasure, and having defaced Thine image, yet being Thy work and creation, wretched though I be, I despair not of my salvation, and dare to approach Thine immeasurable loving-kindness. Accept, then, even me, O Lord, Lover of mankind, as Thou didst accept the sinful woman, the thief, the publican, and the prodigal; and take away the heavy burden of my sins, Thou that takest away the sin of the world, and healest the infirmities of mankind; Who callest the weary and heavy-laden unto Thyself and givest them rest, Who camest not to call the righteous, but sinners to repentance. And do Thou cleanse me from all defilement of flesh and spirit, and teach me to achieve holiness in fear of Thee; that with the pure testimony of my conscience, receiving a portion of Thy Holy Things, I may be united unto Thy holy Body and Blood, and have Thee living and abiding in me with the Father and Thy Holy Spirit. Yea, O Lord Jesus Christ my God, let not the communion of Thine immaculate and life-giving Mysteries be unto me for judgment, neither unto infirmity of soul and body because of my partaking of them unworthily; but grant me until my last breath to receive without condemnation the portion of Thy Holy Things, unto communion with the Holy Spirit, as a provision for life eternal, for an acceptable defence at Thy dread judgment seat; so that I also, with all Thine elect, may become a partaker of Thine incorruptible blessings, which Thou hast prepared for them that love Thee, O Lord, in whom Thou art glorified unto the ages. Amen.

A Prayer of Our Father among the Saints, John Chrysostom, 2:

O Lord My God, I know that I am not worthy nor sufficient that Thou shouldest enter beneath the roof of the temple of my soul, for all is empty and fallen, and Thou hast not in me a place worthy to lay Thy head; but as from on high Thou didst humble Thyself for our sake, do Thou now also lower Thyself to my lowliness; and as Thou didst consent to lie in a cave and in a manger of dumb beasts, so consent also to lie in the manger of mine irrational soul and to enter into my defiled body. And as Thou didst not refuse to enter and to dine with sinners in the house of Simon the Leper, so deign also to enter into the house of my lowly soul, leprous and sinful. And as Thou didst not reject the harlot and sinner like me, when she came and touched Thee, so be compassionate also with me a sinner, as I approach and touch Thee. And as

Thou didst feel no loathing for the defiled and unclean lips of her that kissed Thee, do Thou also not loathe my defiled lips nor mine abominable and impure mouth, and my polluted and unclean tongue. But let the fiery coal of Thy most Holy Body and Thy precious Blood be unto me for sanctification and enlightenment and health for my lowly soul and body, unto the lightening of the burden of my many sins, for preservation from every act of the devil, for the expulsion and prohibition of mine evil and wicked habits, unto the mortification of the passions, unto the keeping of Thy commandments, unto the application of Thy divine grace, unto the acquiring of Thy kingdom. For not with disdain do I approach Thee, O Christ God, but as one trusting in Thine ineffable goodness, and that I may not by much abstaining from Thy communion become the prey of the spiritual wolf. Wherefore do I entreat Thee, for Thou art the only Holy One, O Master: Sanctify my soul and body, my mind and heart, my belly and inward parts, and renew me entirely. And implant Thy fear in my members, and make Thy sanctification inalienable from me, and be unto me a helper and defender, guiding my life in peace, vouchsafing me also to stand at Thy right hand with Thy saints, through the intercessions and supplications of Thy most pure Mother, of Thine immaterial ministers and immaculate hosts, and of all the saints who from the ages have been pleasing unto Thee. Amen.

Another Prayer, of Symeon Metaphrastes, 3:

O only pure and sinless Lord, Who, through the ineffable compassion of Thy love for mankind, didst take on all of our substance from the pure and virgin blood of her that bare Thee supernaturally through the descent of the Divine Spirit and the good will of the everlasting Father; O Christ Jesus, Wisdom of God, and Peace, and Power, Thou Who through the assumption of our nature didst take upon Thyself Thy life-giving and saving Passion–the Cross, the nails, the spear, and death: mortify the soul-corrupting passions of my body. Thou Who by Thy burial didst lead captive the kingdom of hades, bury with good thoughts mine evil schemes, and destroy the spirits of evil. Thou Who by Thy life-bearing Resurrection on the third day didst raise up our fallen forefather, raise me up who have slipped down into sin, setting before me the ways of repentance. Thou Who by Thy most glorious Ascension didst deify the flesh that Thou hadst taken, and didst honour it with a seat at the right hand of the Father, vouchsafe me through partaking of Thy holy Mysteries to obtain a place at Thy right hand among them that are saved. O Thou Who by the descent of Thy Spirit, the Comforter, didst make Thy holy disciples worthy vessels, show me also to be a receptacle of His coming. Thou Who art to come again to judge the world in righteousness, deign to let me also meet Thee on the clouds, my Judge and Creator, with all Thy saints; that I may endlessly glorify and praise Thee, with Thine unoriginate Father, and Thy Most-holy and good and life-creating Spirit, now and ever, and unto the ages of ages. Amen.

Of the divine Damascene, 4:

O Master Lord Jesus Christ our God, Who alone hast authority to remit the sins of men: Do Thou, as the Good One and Lover of mankind, overlook all mine offences, whether committed with knowledge or in ignorance. And vouchsafe me to partake without condemnation of Thy Divine, glorious, immaculate, and life-giving Mysteries; not as a burden, nor for punishment, nor for an increase of sins, but unto purification and sanctification, and as a pledge of the life and kingdom to come, as a bulwark and help, and for the destruction of enemies, and for the blotting out of my many transgressions. For Thou art a God of mercy, and compassion, and love for mankind, and unto Thee do we send up glory, with the Father, and the Holy Spirit, now and ever, and unto the ages of ages. Amen.

Of Basil the Great, 5:

I know, O Lord, that I partake unworthily of Thine immaculate Body and Thy precious Blood, and that I am guilty, and eat and drink damnation to myself, not discerning the Body and Blood of Thee, my Christ and God; but taking courage from Thy compassion I approach Thee Who hast said: He that eateth My Flesh, and drinketh My Blood, abideth in Me and I in him. Show compassion, therefore, O Lord, and do not accuse me, a sinner, but deal with me according to Thy mercy; and let these Holy Things be for me unto healing, and purification, and enlightenment, and preservation, and salvation, and unto sanctification of soul and body; unto the driving away of every phantasy, and evil practice, and activity of the devil working mentally in my members; unto confidence and love toward Thee, unto correction of life, unto steadfastness, unto an increase of virtue and perfection, unto fulfillment of the commandments, unto communion with the Holy Spirit, as a provision for life eternal, as an acceptable defence at Thy dread tribunal, not unto judgment or condemnation.

A Prayer of St. Symeon the New Theologian, 6:
From sullied lips, from an abominable heart, from a tongue impure, from a soul defiled, accept my supplication, O my Christ, and disdain me not, neither my words, nor my ways, nor my shamelessness. Grant me to say boldly that which I desire, O my Christ. Or rather, teach me what I ought to do and say. I have sinned more than the sinful woman who, having learned where Thou wast lodging, bought

myrrh, and came daringly to anoint Thy feet, my God, my Master, and my Christ. As Thou didst not reject her when she drew near from her heart, neither, O Word, be Thou filled with loathing for me, but grant me Thy feet to clasp and kiss, and with floods of tears, as with most precious myrrh, dare to anoint them. Wash me with my tears, and purify me with them, O Word; remit also my transgressions, and grant me pardon. Thou knowest the multitude of mine evils, Thou knowest also my sores, and Thou seest my wounds; but also Thou knowest my faith and Thou beholdest my good intentions, and Thou hearest my sighs. Nothing is hidden from Thee, my God, my Creator, my Redeemer, neither a teardrop, nor a part of a drop. My deeds not yet done Thine eyes have seen, and in Thy book even things not yet accomplished are written by Thee. See my lowliness, see my toil, how great it is, and all my sins take from me, O God of all; that with a pure heart, a trembling mind, and a contrite soul I may partake of Thy spotless and most holy Mysteries, by which all that eat and drink in purity of heart are quickened and deified. For Thou, O my Master, hast said: Everyone that eateth My Flesh and drinketh My Blood abideth in Me, and I in him. True is every word of my Master and God; for whosoever partaketh of the divine and deifying grace is no more alone, but with Thee, my Christ, the three-sunned Light that enlighteneth the world. And that I may not remain alone without Thee, the Life-giver, my Breath, my Life, my Rejoicing, the Salvation of the world, therefore have I drawn nigh unto Thee, as Thou seest, with tears, and with a contrite soul. O Ransom of mine offences, I ask Thee to receive me, and that I may partake without condemnation of Thy life-giving and perfect Mysteries, that Thou mayest remain, as Thou hast said, with me, a thrice-wretched one, lest the deceiver, finding me without Thy grace, craftily seize me, and having beguiled me, draw me away from Thy deifying words. Wherefore, I fall down before Thee, and fervently cry unto Thee: As Thou did receive the prodigal, and the sinful woman who drew near, so receive me, the prodigal and profligate, O Compassionate One. With contrite soul I now come to Thee. I know, O Saviour, that none other hath sinned against Thee as have I, nor hath wrought the deeds that I have done. But this again I know, that neither the magnitude of mine offences nor the multitude of my sins surpasseth the abundant long-suffering of my God and His exceeding love for mankind; but with sympathetic mercy Thou dost purify and illumine them that fervently repent, and makest them partakers of the light, sharers of Thy divinity without stint. And, strange to angels and to the minds of men, Thou conversest with them oftimes, as with Thy true friends. These things make me bold, these things give me wings, O Christ. And taking courage from the wealth of Thy benefactions to us, rejoicing and trembling at once, I partake of Fire, I that am grass. And, strange wonder! I am bedewed without being consumed, as the bush of old burned without being consumed. Now with thankful mind, and grateful heart, with thankfulness in my members, my soul and body, I worship and magnify and glorify Thee, my God, for blessed art Thou, both now and unto the ages.

Another Prayer of Chrysostom, 7:

O God, loose, remit, and pardon me my transgressions wherein I have sinned against Thee, whether by word, deed, or thought, voluntarily or involuntarily, consciously or unconsciously; forgive me all, for Thou art good and the Lover of mankind. And through the intercessions of Thy most pure Mother, Thy noetic ministers and holy hosts, and all the saints who from the ages have been pleasing unto Thee, deign to allow me without condemnation to receive Thy holy and immaculate Body and precious Blood, unto the healing of soul and body, and unto the purification of mine evil thoughts. For Thine is the kingdom, and the power, and the glory, with the Father and the Holy Spirit, now and ever, and unto the ages of ages. Amen.

Of the same, 8:

I am not sufficient, O Master and Lord, that Thou shouldst enter under the roof of my soul; but as Thou dost will as the Lover of mankind to dwell in me, I dare to approach Thee. Thou commandest: I shall open the doors which Thou alone didst create, that

Thou mayest enter with Thy love for mankind, as is Thy nature, that Thou mayest enter and enlighten my darkened thought. I believe that Thou wilt do this, for Thou didst not drive away the sinful woman when she came unto Thee with tears, neither didst Thou reject the publican who repented, nor didst Thou spurn the thief who acknowledged Thy kingdom, nor didst Thou leave the repentant persecutor to himself; but all of them that came unto Thee in repentance Thou didst number among Thy friends, O Thou Who alone art blessed, always, now and unto endless ages. Amen.

Of the same, 9:

O Lord Jesus Christ my God, loose, remit, cleanse, and forgive me, Thy sinful and unprofitable, and unworthy servant, my transgressions and offences and fallings into sin, which I have committed against Thee from my youth until the present day and hour, whether consciously or unconsciously, whether by words or deeds, or in thought or imagination, in habit, and in all my senses. And through the intercessions of her that seedlessly gave

Thee birth, the most pure and Ever-Virgin Mary, Thy Mother, the only hope that maketh not ashamed, and my mediation and salvation, vouchsafe me without condemnation to partake of Thine immaculate, immortal, life-giving and awesome Mysteries, unto the remission of sins and for life eternal, unto sanctification and enlightenment, strength, healing, and health of both soul and body, and unto the consumption and complete destruction of mine evil reasonings and intentions and prejudices and nocturnal phantasies of dark and evil spirits; for Thine is the kingdom, and the power, and the glory, and the honour and the worship, with the Father and Thy Holy Spirit, now and ever, and unto the ages of ages. Amen.

Another Prayer of John Damascene, 10:

I stand before the doors of Thy temple, yet I do not put away evil thoughts. But do Thou, O Christ God, Who didst justify the publican, and didst have mercy on the woman of Canaan, and didst open the doors of paradise to the thief, open unto me the abyss of Thy love for mankind, and receive me as I come and touch Thee, as Thou didst receive the sinful woman and the woman with an issue of blood. For the one received healing easily by touching the hem of Thy garment, while the other, by clasping Thy most pure feet, carried away absolution of sins. And I, a wretch, daring to receive Thy whole Body, let me not be consumed by fire; but receive me, as Thou didst receive them, and enlighten my spiritual, senses, burning up my sinful errors; through the intercessions of her that seedlessly gave Thee birth, and of the heavenly hosts, for blessed art Thou unto the ages of ages. Amen.

Another Prayer of Chrysostom:

I believe, O Lord and I confess that Thou art truly the Christ, the Son of the living God, Who came into the world to save sinners, of whom I am chief. Moreover, I believe that this is truly Thy most pure Body and this is truly Thine Own precious Blood; wherefore I pray thee: Have mercy on me and forgive me my transgressions, voluntary and involuntary, whether in word or deed, in knowledge or in ignorance. And vouchsafe me to partake without condemnation Thy most pure Mysteries, unto the remission of sins and life everlasting. Amen.

When coming to partake, say to oneself these lines of Metaphrastes:

Behold, I approach the Divine Communion.

O Creator, let me not be burnt by communicating,

For Thou art Fire, consuming the unworthy.

But, rather, purify me of all impurity.

Then again say:

Of Thy Mystical Supper, O Son of God, receive me today as a communicant; for I will not speak of the Mystery to Thine enemies; nor will I give Thee a kiss, as did Judas, but like the thief do I confess Thee: Remember me, O Lord, in Thy kingdom.

Again these lines:

Be awe-stricken, O mortal, beholding the deifying Blood;

For It is a fire that consumeth the unworthy.

The Divine Body both deifieth and nourisheth me.

It deifieth the spirit, and wondrously nourisheth the mind.

Then the Troparia:

Thou hast sweetened me with Thy love, O Christ, and by Thy Divine zeal hast Thou changed me. But do Thou consume my sins with immaterial fire, and vouchsafe me to be filled with delight in Thee; that, leaping for joy, O Good One, I may magnify Thy two comings.

Into the brilliant company of Thy saints how shall I the unworthy enter? For if I dare to enter into the bridechamber, my garment betrayeth me, for it is not a wedding garment, and I shall be bound and cast out by the angels. Cleanse, O Lord, my soul of pollution, and save me, as Thou art the Lover of mankind.

Then the Prayer:

O Master, Lover of mankind, O Lord Jesus Christ my God, let not these Holy Things be unto me for judgment, through my being unworthy, but unto the purification and sanctification of soul and body, and as a pledge of the life and kingdom to come. For it is good for me to cleave unto God, to put my hope of salvation in the Lord.

And again:

Of Thy Mystical Supper, O Son of God, receive me today as a communicant; for I will not speak of the Mystery to Thine enemies; nor will I give Thee a kiss, as did Judas; but like the thief do I confess Thee: Remember me, O Lord, in Thy kingdom.

THE END OF THE PRE-COMMUNION PRAYERS

Deacon: Bless, master. *(Said only if a deacon serve)*

Priest: Blessed is the kingdom of the Father, and of the Son, and of the Holy Spirit, now and ever, and unto the ages of ages.

CHOIR: Amen.

Deacon (Priest): In peace let us pray to the Lord.

CHOIR: Lord, have mercy.

Deacon (Priest): For the peace from above, and the salvation of our souls, let us pray to the Lord.

CHOIR: Lord, have mercy.

Deacon (Priest): For the peace of the whole world, the good estate of the holy churches of God, and the union of all, let us pray to the Lord.

CHOIR: Lord, have mercy.

Deacon (Priest): For this holy temple, and for them that with faith, reverence, and the fear of God enter herein, let us pray to the Lord.

CHOIR: Lord, have mercy.

Deacon (Priest): For the Orthodox episcopate of the Church of Russia; for our lord the Very Most Reverend Metropolitan *N.*, First Hierarch of the Russian Church Abroad; for our lord the Most Reverend (Archbishop *or* Bishop *N., whose diocese it is)*; for the venerable priesthood, the diaconate in Christ, for all the clergy and people, let us pray to the Lord.

CHOIR: Lord, have mercy.

Deacon (Priest): For the suffering Russian land and its Orthodox people both in the homeland and in the diaspora, and for their salvation, let us pray to the Lord.

CHOIR: Lord, have mercy.

Deacon (Priest): For this land, its authorities and armed forces, let us pray to the Lord.

CHOIR: Lord, have mercy,

Deacon (Priest): That He may deliver His people from enemies visible and invisible, and confirm in us oneness of mind, brotherly love, and piety, let us pray to the Lord.

CHOIR: Lord, have mercy.

Deacon (Priest): For this city, (*or* town, *or* holy monastery), for every city and country, and the faithful that dwell therein, let us pray to the Lord.

CHOIR: Lord, have mercy.

Deacon (Priest): For seasonable weather, abundance of the fruits of the earth, and peaceful times, let us pray to the Lord.

CHOIR: Lord, have mercy.

Deacon (Priest): For travelers by sea, land, and air; for the sick, the suffering, the imprisoned, and for their salvation, let us pray to the Lord.

CHOIR: Lord, have mercy.

Deacon (Priest): That we may be delivered from all tribulation, wrath, and necessity, let us pray to the Lord.

CHOIR: Lord, have mercy.

Deacon (Priest): Help us, save us, have mercy on us, and keep us, O God, by Thy grace.

CHOIR: Lord, have mercy.

Deacon (Priest): Calling to remembrance our most holy, most pure, most blessed, glorious Lady Theotokos and Ever-Virgin Mary with all the saints, let us commit ourselves and one another and all our life unto Christ our God.

CHOIR: To Thee, O Lord. (*Slowly, if there*

be no deacon)

Priest: For unto Thee is due all glory, honour, and worship: to the Father, and to the Son, and to the Holy Spirit, now and ever, and unto the ages of ages.

CHOIR: Amen. *And they chant the First Antiphon, Psalm 102. For the abridged form, see page 63.*

Bless the Lord, O my soul; blessed art Thou, O Lord.* Bless the Lord, O my soul, and all that is within me bless His holy name.* Bless the Lord, O my soul, and forget not all that He hath done for thee.* Who is gracious unto all thine iniquities,* Who healeth all thine infirmities.* Who redeemeth thy life from corruption, Who crowneth thee with mercy and compassion.* Who fulfilleth thy desire with good things; thy youth shall be renewed as the eagle's.* The Lord performeth deeds of mercy, and executeth judgment for all them that are wronged. He hath made His ways known unto Moses, unto the sons of Israel the things that He hath willed.* Compassionate and merciful is the Lord, long-suffering and plenteous in mercy.* Not unto the end will He be angered, neither unto eternity will He be wroth. Not according to our iniquities hath He dealt with us, neither according to our sins hath He rewarded us. * For according to the height of heaven from the earth, the Lord hath made His mercy to prevail over them that fear Him. * As far as the east is from the west, so far hath He removed our iniquities from us. * Like as a father hath compassion upon His sons, so hath the Lord had compassion upon them that fear Him; * for He knoweth whereof we are made, He hath remembered that we are dust. * As for man, his days are as the grass; as a flower of the field, so shall he blossom forth. * For when the wind is passed over it, then it shall be gone, and no longer will it know the place thereof. * But the mercy of the Lord is from eternity, even unto eternity, upon them that fear Him. * And His righteousness is upon sons of sons, upon them that keep His testament and remember His commandments to do them. * The Lord in heaven hath prepared His throne, and His kingdom ruleth over all. * Bless the Lord, all ye His angels, mighty in strength, that perform

His word, to hear the voice of His words.* Bless the Lord, all ye His hosts, His ministers that do His will.* Bless the Lord, all ye His works, in every place of His dominion.

Glory to the Father,* and to the Son,* and to the Holy Spirit. Both now and ever,* and unto the ages of ages. Amen.

Bless the Lord, O my soul,* and all that is within me* bless His holy name;* blessed art Thou, O Lord.

In the parishes it is often the custom to chant only the following:

Bless the Lord, O my soul;* blessed art Thou, O Lord.* Bless the Lord, O my soul,* and all that is within* me bless His holy name.* Bless the Lord, O my soul,* and forget not all that He hath done for thee.* Who is gracious unto all thine iniquities,* Who healeth all thine infirmities.* Who redeemeth thy life from corruption,* Who crowneth thee with mercy and compassion.* Who fulfilleth thy desire with good things;* thy youth shall be renewed as the eagle's.* Compassionate and merciful is the Lord,* long-suffering and plenteous in mercy.

Glory to the Father,* and to the Son,* and to the Holy Spirit;

Both now and ever,* and unto the ages of ages. Amen.

Bless the Lord, O my soul,* and all that is within me* bless His holy name;* blessed art Thou, Lord.

Deacon (Priest): Again and again, in peace let us pray to the Lord.

CHOIR: Lord, have mercy.

Deacon (Priest): Help us, save us, have mercy on us, and keep us, O God, by Thy grace.

CHOIR: Lord, have mercy.

Deacon (Priest): Calling to remembrance our most holy, most pure, most blessed, glorious Lady Theotokos and Ever-Virgin Mary with all the saints, let us commit ourselves and one another and all our life unto Christ our God.

CHOIR: To Thee, O Lord.

Priest: For Thine is the dominion, and Thine is the kingdom, and the power, and the glory: of the Father, and of the Son, and of the Holy Spirit, now and ever, and unto the ages of ages.

CHOIR: Amen. *And they chant the Second*

Antiphon, Psalm 145:

Glory to the Father, * and to the Son, * and to the Holy Spirit.

Praise the Lord, O my soul. * I will praise the Lord in my life, * I will chant unto my God for as long as I have my being. * Trust ye not in princes, in the sons of men, * in whom there is no salvation, * His spirit shall go forth, * and he shall return unto his earth. * In that day all his thoughts shall perish. * Blessed is he of whom the God of Jacob is his help, * whose hope is in the Lord his God. * Who hath made heaven and the earth, * the sea and all that is therein. * Who keepeth truth unto eternity, * Who executeth judgment for the wronged, * Who giveth food unto the hungry. * The Lord looseth the fettered; * the Lord maketh wise the blind; * the Lord setteth aright the fallen; * the Lord loveth the righteous; * The Lord preserveth the proselytes. * He shall adopt for His own the orphan and widow, * and the way of sinners shall He destroy. * The Lord shall be king unto eternity; * thy God, O Sion, unto generation and generation.

Both now and ever, and unto the ages of

ages. *Amen.*

O Only-begotten Son and Word of God, Who art immortal, * yet didst deign for our salvation * to be incarnate of the holy Theotokos and Ever-Virgin Mary, * and without change didst become man, * and wast crucified, O Christ God, trampling down death by death, * Thou Who art one of the Holy Trinity, * glorified with the Father and the Holy Spirit, save us.

Deacon (Priest): Again and again, in peace let us pray to the Lord.

CHOIR: Lord, have mercy.

Deacon (Priest): Help us, save us, have mercy on us, and keep us, O God, by Thy grace.

CHOIR: Lord, have mercy.

Deacon (Priest): Calling to remembrance our most holy, most pure, most blessed, glorious Lady Theotokos and Ever-Virgin Mary with all the saints, let us commit ourselves and one another and all our life unto Christ our God.

CHOIR: To Thee, O Lord.

Priest: For a good God art Thou, and the Lover of mankind, and unto Thee do we send up glory: to the Father, and to the Son, and to the Holy Spirit, now and ever, and unto the ages of ages.

CHOIR: Amen. *And they chant the Third Antiphon, the Beatitudes:*

In Thy kingdom remember us, O Lord, * when Thou comest in Thy kingdom.

Blessed are the poor in spirit, * for theirs is the kingdom of heaven.

Blessed are they that mourn, * for they shall be comforted.

Blessed are the meek, * for they shall inherit the earth.

Blessed are they that hunger and thirst after righteousness, * for they shall be filled.

Blessed are the merciful, * for they shall obtain mercy.

Blessed are the pure in heart, * for they shall see God.

Blessed are the peacemakers, * for they shall be called sons of God.

Blessed are they that are persecuted for righteousness' sake, * for theirs is the kingdom of heaven.

Blessed are ye when men shall revile you and persecute you, * and shall say all manner of evil against you falsely for My sake.

Rejoice and be exceeding glad,* for great is your reward in the heavens.

Glory to the Father,* and to the Son,* and to the Holy Spirit;

Both now and ever,* and unto the ages of ages. Amen.

THE SMALL ENTRY

Deacon (Priest): Wisdom! Aright!

CHOIR: (Clergy first, if a bishop serve, with Choir beginning at O Son of God...): O come let us worship and fall down before Christ; O Son of God (*Sundays:* Who didst rise from the dead) (*on feasts of the Theotokos:* through the prayers of the Theotokos) (*On weekdays:* Who art wondrous in the saints), save us who chant unto Thee: Alleluia, alleluia, alleluia.

Then the appointed troparia and kontakia are chanted. See pages 110-276.

Priest (Bishop): For holy art Thou, O our God, and unto Thee do we send up glory: to the Father, and to the Son, and to the Holy Spirit, now and ever: (*if there be neither bishop or deacon serving, the priest addeth*) and unto the ages of ages.

And if there be a deacon, but no bishop serving:
Deacon: O Lord, save the pious, and hearken unto us.
CHOIR: O Lord, save the pious, and hearken unto us.
Deacon: And unto the ages of ages.
CHOIR: Amen.
Holy God, Holy Mighty, Holy Immortal, have mercy on us. *Thrice.*
Glory to the Father, and to the Son, and to the Holy Spirit, both now and ever, and unto the ages of ages. Holy Immortal, have mercy on us.
Holy God, Holy Mighty, Holy Immortal, have mercy on us.

But if a bishop serve:
Deacon: O Lord, save the pious:
CHOIR: O Lord, save the pious:
Deacon: And hearken unto us.
CHOIR: And hearken unto us.
Deacon: And unto the ages of ages.
CHOIR: Amen. *And the Trisagion:*
If a bishop serve, the Trisagion is done thus:
CHOIR: Holy God, Holy Mighty, Holy Immortal, have mercy on us. *Once.*

Clergy: Holy God, Holy Mighty, Holy Immortal, have mercy on us. *Once.*

CHOIR: Holy God, Holy Mighty, Holy Immortal, have mercy on us. *Once, rapidly.*

Bishop: Lord, O Lord, look down from heaven and behold and visit this vineyard, and perfect that which Thy right hand hath planted. (*or he may say merely:* Holy God. *And he blesseth with the Cross and the dikirion.*)

CHOIR: Holy God. *And the bishop repeateth the above in a different language, if he chooseth; otherwise he saith:* Holy Mighty.

CHOIR: Holy Mighty. *And the bishop may repeat the above in a third language, or he saith:* Holy Immortal, have mercy on us.

CHOIR: Holy Immortal, have mercy on us.

Then, CHOIR: Holy God, Holy Mighty, Holy Immortal, have mercy on us. *Once, rapidly.*

Clergy: Holy God, Holy Mighty, Holy Immortal, have mercy on us. *Once.*

CHOIR: Glory to the Father, and to the Son, and to the Holy Spirit, both now and ever, and unto the ages of ages. Amen. Holy Immortal, have mercy on us.

Holy God, Holy Mighty, Holy Immortal,

have mercy on us.

THE EPISTLE

Deacon (Priest): Let us attend,

Priest (Bishop): Peace be unto all.

Reader (Deacon): And to thy spirit.

Deacon (Priest): Wisdom!

Reader (Deacon): The Prokeimenon in the __Tone. *And he giveth the words of the prokei-menon (pp.110-276). If there be two prokeimena, the first one is chanted twice and the second one once.*

Deacon (Priest): Wisdom!

Reader (Deacon): The Reading is from ____ (the Acts of the Holy Apostles) (the catholic Epistle of____) (the Epistle of the holy Apostle Paul to the ____, *or* to Timothy, *etc.*)

Deacon (Priest): Let us attend.

Reader (Deacon): In those days, (*if from Acts*); Beloved, (*if from I, II, or III John*); Breth-ren, or Child Timothy, *etc. (if from the Epistles of the Apostle Paul), and the reading. When the reader is finished:*

Priest (Bishop): Peace be unto thee.

Reader (Deacon): And to thy spirit.

Deacon (Priest): Wisdom!

Reader (Deacon): Alleluia in the ___ Tone.

CHOIR: Alleluia, alleluia, alleluia.

Reader (Deacon), stichos.

CHOIR: Alleluia, alleluia, alleluia.

Reader (Deacon), stichos.

CHOIR: Alleluia, alleluia, alleluia.

THE GOSPEL

If a deacon serve, Deacon: Bless, master, the bringer of the Good Tidings of the holy Apostle and Evangelist *N.*

Priest (Bishop): May God, through the intercessions of the holy glorious, all-praised Apostle and Evangelist *N.*, give speech with great power unto thee that bringest good tidings, unto the fulfillment of the Gospel of His beloved Son, our Lord Jesus Christ.

Deacon (Priest): Wisdom! Aright! Let us hear the Holy Gospel.

Priest (Bishop): Peace be unto all.

CHOIR: And to thy spirit.

Deacon (Priest): The Reading is from the Holy Gospel according to *N.*

CHOIR: Glory to Thee, O Lord, glory to Thee.

Deacon (Priest): Let us attend. *And the Gospel.*

If a deacon read the Gospel, when he is finished, the priest (or bishop) saith: Peace be unto thee that bringest good tidings.

CHOIR: Glory to Thee, O Lord, glory to Thee.

THE AUGMENTED ECTENIA

Deacon (Priest): Let us all say with our whole soul and with our whole mind, let us say.

CHOIR: Lord, have mercy.

Deacon (Priest): O Lord Almighty, the God of our fathers, we pray Thee, hearken and have mercy.

CHOIR: Lord, have mercy.

Deacon (Priest): Have mercy on us, O God, according to Thy great mercy, we pray Thee, hearken and have mercy.

CHOIR: Lord, have mercy. *Thrice.*

Deacon (Priest): Again we pray for the Orthodox episcopate of the Church of Russia; for our lord the Very Most Reverend Metropolitan *N.,* First Hierarch of the Russian Church Abroad; for our lord the Most Reverend (Archbishop *or* Bishop *N., whose diocese it is);* and all our brethren in Christ.

CHOIR: Lord, have mercy. *Thrice.*

Deacon (Priest): Again we pray for the suffering Russian land and its Orthodox people both in the homeland and in the diaspora and for their salvation.

CHOIR: Lord, have mercy. *Thrice.*

Deacon (Priest): Again we pray for this land, its authorities and armed forces.

CHOIR: Lord, have mercy. *Thrice.*

Deacon (Priest): Again we pray that to the Lord our God that He may deliver His people from enemies visible and invisible, and confirm in us oneness of mind, brotherly love, and piety.

CHOIR: Lord, have mercy. *Thrice.*

Deacon (Priest): Again we pray for our brethren, the priests, priestmonks, and all our brethren in Christ.

CHOIR: Lord, have mercy. *Thrice.*

Deacon (Priest): Again we pray for the blessed and ever-memorable, holy Orthodox patriarchs; for pious kings and right-believing queens; and for the founders of this holy temple (*or* this holy monastery), and for our fathers and brethren gone to their rest before us, and the Orthodox here and everywhere laid to rest.

CHOIR: Lord, have mercy. *Thrice.*

Here may be inserted various additional petitions, i.e., for the ill and afflicted, the newly-baptized, etc.

Deacon (Priest): Again we pray for them that bring offerings and do good works in this holy and all-venerable temple; for them that minister and them that chant, and for all the people here present that await of Thee great and abundant mercy.

CHOIR: Lord, have mercy. *Thrice.*

Priest (Bishop): For a merciful God art Thou, and the Lover of mankind, and unto Thee do we send up glory: to the Father, and to the Son, and to the Holy Spirit, now and ever, and unto the ages of ages.

CHOIR: Amen.

The Prayer for the Salvation of Russia
(Usually omitted on great feasts)

Deacon (Priest): Let us pray to the Lord.

CHOIR: Lord, have mercy. *Slowly.*

Priest (Bishop):

O Lord Jesus Christ our God: Accept from us, Thine unworthy servants, this fervent supplication, and, having forgiven us all our sins, remember all our enemies that hate and wrong us, and render not unto them according to their deeds, but according to Thy great mercy convert them: the unbelieving to true faith and piety, and the believing that they may turn away from evil and do good. By Thine all-powerful might, mercifully deliver all of us and Thy holy Church and the suffering land of Russia from every evil circumstance. Hearken unto the painful cry of Thy faithful servants who cry unto Thee day and night in tribulation and sorrow, O our most merciful God, and lead their life out of corruption. Grant peace and tranquility, love and steadfastness, and swift reconciliation to Thy people, whom Thou hast redeemed by Thy precious Blood. But unto them that have departed from Thee and seek Thee not, be Thou manifest, that not one of them perish, but that all of them be saved and come to the knowledge of the truth; that all in harmonious oneness of mind and unceasing love may glorify

Thy most holy name, O patient-hearted Lord Who art quick to forgive, unto the ages of ages.

CHOIR: Amen.

THE ECTENIA FOR THE DEPARTED

(Not said on Sundays and feasts)

Deacon (Priest): Have mercy on us, O God, according to Thy great mercy, we pray Thee, hearken and have mercy.

CHOIR: Lord, have mercy. *Thrice.*

Deacon (Priest): Again we pray for the repose of the souls of the departed servants of God, *N.,N.,* and that they may be forgiven every transgression, both voluntary and involuntary.

CHOIR: Lord, have mercy. *Thrice.*

Deacon (Priest): That the Lord God commit their souls to where the righteous repose.

CHOIR: Lord, have mercy. *Thrice.*

Deacon (Priest): The mercy of God, the kingdom of heaven, and the remission of their sins, let us ask of Christ the immortal King and our God.

CHOIR: Grant this, O Lord.

Deacon (Priest): Let us pray to the Lord.

CHOIR: Lord, have mercy.

Priest: For Thou art the resurrection, and the life, and the repose of Thy departed servants, *N., N.,* O Christ our God, and unto Thee do we send up glory, together with Thine unoriginate Father, and Thy Most-holy, and good and life-creating Spirit, now and ever, and unto the ages of ages.

CHOIR: Amen.

THE ECTENIA OF THE CATECHUMENS

Deacon (Priest): Pray, ye catechumens, to the Lord.

CHOIR: Lord, have mercy.

Deacon (Priest): Ye faithful, for the catechumens let us pray, that the Lord will have mercy on them.

CHOIR: Lord, have mercy.

Deacon (Priest): That He will catechize them with the word of Truth.

CHOIR: Lord, have mercy.

Deacon (Priest): That He will reveal unto them the Gospel of righteousness.

CHOIR: Lord, have mercy

Deacon (Priest): That He will unite them to His Holy, Catholic, and Apostolic Church.

CHOIR: Lord, have mercy.

Deacon (Priest): Save them, have mercy on them, help them, and keep them, O God, by Thy grace.

CHOIR: Lord, have mercy.

Deacon (Priest): Ye catechumens, bow your heads to the Lord.

CHOIR: To Thee, O Lord. (*Slowly, if there be no deacon serving.*)

Priest: That they also with us may glorify Thy most honourable and majestic name: of the Father, and of the Son, and of the Holy Spirit, now and ever, and unto the ages of ages.

CHOIR: Amen.

THE ECTENIA OF THE FAITHFUL

Deacon (Priest): As many as are catechumens, depart; catechumens, depart; as many as are catechumens, depart; let none of the catechumens remain; as many as are of the faithful, again and again, in peace let us pray to the Lord.

CHOIR: Lord, have mercy. (*Slowly, if there be no deacon.*)

Deacon (Priest): Help us, save us, have mercy

on us, and keep us, O God, by Thy grace.

CHOIR: Lord, have mercy.

Deacon (Priest): Wisdom!

Priest: For unto Thee is due all glory, honour, and worship: to the Father, and to the Son, and to the Holy Spirit, now and ever, and unto the ages of ages.

CHOIR: Amen.

Deacon (Priest): Again and again, in peace let us pray to the Lord.

CHOIR: Lord, have mercy. (*Slowly, if there be no deacon.*)

If there be no deacon, the following four petitions are not said.

Deacon: For the peace from above, and the salvation of our souls, let us pray to the Lord.

CHOIR: Lord, have mercy.

Deacon: For the peace of the whole world, the good estate of the holy churches of God, and the union of all, let us pray to the Lord

CHOIR: Lord, have mercy.

Deacon: For this holy temple, and for them that with faith, reverence, and the fear of God enter herein, let us pray to the Lord.

CHOIR: Lord, have mercy.

Deacon: That we may be delivered from all tribulation, wrath, and necessity, let us pray to the Lord.

CHOIR: Lord, have mercy.

Deacon (Priest): Help us, save us, have mercy on us, and keep us, O God, by Thy grace.

CHOIR: Lord, have mercy. (*Slowly, if there be no deacon.*)

Deacon (Priest): Wisdom!

Priest (Bishop): That always being guarded under Thy dominion, we may send up glory unto Thee: to the Father, and to the Son, and to the Holy Spirit, now and ever, and unto the ages of ages.

CHOIR: Amen.

THE CHERUBIC HYMN

CHOIR: Let us who mystically represent the Cherubim, and chant the thrice-holy hymn unto the Life-creating Trinity, now lay aside all earthly care.

THE GREAT ENTRY

(*If a bishop serve, the deacon commemorateth only him, and the bishop saith all the remaining commemorations.*)

Deacon (Priest): The Orthodox episcopate

of the Church of Russia; our lord the Very Most Reverend *N.*, Metropolitan of Eastern America and New York, and First Hierarch of the Russian Church Abroad; and our lord the Most Reverend (Archbishop *or* Bishop *N.*, *whose diocese it is*), may the Lord God remember in His kingdom, always, now and ever, and unto the ages of ages.

Priest: The suffering Russian land and its Orthodox people both in the homeland and in the diaspora, this land, its authorities and the faithful that dwell therein, may the Lord God remember in His kingdom, always, now and ever, and unto the ages of ages.

The clergy, the monastics, all that are persecuted and suffer for the Orthodox Faith; the founders, benefactors, and the brotherhood of this holy temple (*or* monastery), and all of you Orthodox Christians, may the Lord God remember in His kingdom, always, now and ever, and unto the ages of ages.

CHOIR: Amen. That we may receive the King of all, Who cometh invisibly upborne in triumph by the ranks of angels. Alleluia, alleluia, alleluia.

ECTENIA OF FERVENT SUPPLICATION

Deacon (Priest): Let us complete our prayer unto the Lord.

CHOIR: Lord, have mercy.

Deacon (Priest): For the precious gifts set forth, let us pray to the Lord.

CHOIR: Lord, have mercy.

Deacon (Priest): For this holy temple, and for them that with faith, reverence, and the fear of God enter herein, let us pray to the Lord.

CHOIR: Lord, have mercy.

Deacon (Priest): That we may be delivered from all tribulation, wrath, and necessity, let us pray to the Lord.

CHOIR: Lord, have mercy. (*Slowly, if there be no deacon.*)

Deacon (Priest): Help us, save us, have mercy on us, and keep us, O God, by Thy grace.

CHOIR: Lord, have mercy.

Deacon (Priest): That the whole day may be perfect, holy, peaceful, and sinless, let us ask of the Lord.

CHOIR: Grant this, O Lord.

Deacon (Priest): An angel of peace, a faithful guide, a guardian of our souls and bodies, let us ask of the Lord.

CHOIR: Grant this, O Lord.

Deacon (Priest): Pardon and remission of our sins and offences, let us ask of the Lord.

CHOIR: Grant this, O Lord.

Deacon (Priest): Things good and profitable for our souls, and peace for the world, let us ask of the Lord.

CHOIR: Grant this, O Lord.

Deacon (Priest): That we may complete the remaining time of our life in peace and repentance, let us ask of the Lord.

CHOIR: Grant this, O Lord.

Deacon (Priest): A Christian ending to our life, painless, blameless, peaceful, and a good defense before the dread judgment seat of Christ, let us ask.

CHOIR: Grant this, O Lord.

Deacon (Priest): Calling to remembrance our most holy, most pure, most blessed, glorious Lady Theotokos and Ever Virgin Mary with all the saints, let us commit ourselves and one another and all our life unto Christ our God.

CHOIR: To Thee, O Lord.

Priest: Through the compassions of Thine Only-begotten Son, with Whom Thou art blessed, together with Thy Most-holy, and good, and life-creating Spirit, now and ever, and unto the ages of ages.

CHOIR: Amen.

Priest (Bishop): Peace be unto all.

CHOIR: And to thy spirit.

Deacon (Priest): Let us love one another, that with one mind we may confess:

CHOIR: The Father, and the Son, and the Holy Spirit: the Trinity, one in essence and indivisible.

Deacon (Priest): The doors! The doors! In wisdom let us attend.

CHOIR (*and People*): I believe in one God, the Father Almighty,* Maker of heaven and earth, and of all things visible and invisible.* And in one Lord Jesus Christ, the Son of God,* the Only-begotten, begotten of the Father before all ages;* Light of Light, true God of true God;* begotten, not made; of one essence with the Father; by Whom all things were made;* Who for us men, and for our salvation, came down from the heavens,* and was incarnate of the Holy Spirit and the Virgin Mary, and became man;* And was crucified for us under Pontius Pilate,* and suffered, and was buried; and arose again on the third day according to the Scriptures;* And ascended into the heavens, and sitteth at the right hand of the Father;* And shall come again, with glory, to judge both the living and the dead; Whose kingdom shall have no end.* And in the Holy Spirit, the Lord, the Giver of life; Who proceedeth from the Father;* Who with the Father and the Son together is worshipped and glorified; Who spake by the prophets.* In One, Holy, Catholic, and Apostolic Church.* I confess one baptism for the remission of sins.* I look for the resurrection of the dead,* And the life of the age to come. Amen.

THE ANAPHORA

Deacon (Priest): Let us stand well. let us stand with fear, let us attend, that we may offer the holy oblation in peace.

CHOIR: A mercy of peace, a sacrifice of praise.

Priest (Bishop): The grace of our Lord Jesus Christ, and the love of God the Father, and the communion of the Holy Spirit be with you all.

CHOIR: And with thy spirit.

Priest (Bishop): Let us lift up our hearts.

CHOIR: We lift them up unto the Lord.

Priest (Bishop): Let us give thanks unto the Lord.

CHOIR: It is meet and right to worship the Father, and the Son, and the Holy Spirit: the Trinity, one in essence and indivisible.

Priest (Bishop): Singing the triumphal hymn, shouting, crying aloud, and saying:

CHOIR: Holy, Holy, Holy, Lord of Sabaoth: heaven and earth are full of Thy glory. Hosanna in the highest! Blessed is He that cometh in the name of the Lord. Hosanna in the highest!

If it be the Liturgy of St. John Chrysostom:

Priest (Bishop): Take, eat: this is My Body, which is broken for you for the remission of sins.

CHOIR: Amen.

Priest (Bishop): Drink of it, all of you: this is My Blood of the New Testament, which is shed for you and for many, for the remission of sins.

CHOIR: Amen.

But if it be the Liturgy of St. Basil the Great (January 1, first five Sundays of Lent, Great Thursday and Saturday, and Nativity and Theophany Eves (unless they fall on Saturday or Sunday)):

Priest (Bishop): He gave it to His holy disciples and apostles, saying: Take, eat: this is My Body, which is broken for you for the remission of sins.

CHOIR: Amen.

Priest (Bishop): He gave it to His holy disciples and apostles, saying: Drink of it, all of you: this is My Blood of the New Testament, which is shed for you and for many, for the remission of sins.

CHOIR: Amen.

Priest (Bishop): Thine Own of Thine Own we offer unto Thee, in behalf of all and for all.

CHOIR: We praise Thee, we bless Thee, we give thanks unto Thee, O Lord; and we pray unto Thee, O our God.

Priest (Bishop): Especially for our most holy, most pure, most blessed, glorious Lady Theotokos and Ever-Virgin Mary.

If it be the Liturgy of St. John Chrysostom:

CHOIR: It is truly meet to bless thee, the Theotokos, ever-blessed and most blameless, and Mother of our God. More honourable than the Cherubim, and beyond compare more glorious than the Seraphim, who without corruption gavest birth to God the Word, the very Theotokos, thee do we magnify.

But if it be the Liturgy of St. Basil the Great:

CHOIR: In thee rejoiceth, O thou who art full of grace, all creation, the angelic assembly, and the race of man; O sanctified temple and noetical paradise, praise of virgins, of whom God was incarnate, and became a child, He that was before the ages, even our God; for of thy body a throne He made, and thy womb more spacious than the heavens did He form. In thee rejoiceth, O thou who art full of grace, all creation: glory to thee.

Or, on the Great feasts, the appointed megaly-narion.

If it be a hierarchal liturgy, the deacon, coming out the holy doors, faceth the people, saying.

And each and every one.

CHOIR: And each and every one.

Priest (Bishop, if hierarchal liturgy): Among

the first, remember, O Lord the Orthodox episcopate of the Church of Russia; and our lord the Very Most Reverend Metropolitan *N.*, First Hierarch of the Russian Church Abroad; and our lord the Most Reverend (Archbishop(s) *N.(N.,) or* Bishop(s) *N.(N.,) (naming any other bishops present, but not naming himself),* whom do Thou grant unto Thy holy churches, in peace, safety, honour, health, and length of days, rightly dividing the word of Thy truth.

CHOIR *(if it be not a hierarchal liturgy):* And each and every one. *Then go to bottom of page 91.*

And if it be a hierarchal liturgy, the deacon entereth the holy doors, saying as he goeth:

And our lord the Most Reverend (Archbishop *or* Bishop *N., whose diocese it is) (or the senior bishop serving)* offering these Holy Gifts (*which the deacon indicateth with his right hand as he walketh past the Holy Table on the right side*) to the Lord our God.

And he boweth toward the High Place, and coming out the holy doors he faceth the people, saying:

For the honourable priesthood and for the diaconate in Christ, and for all those in the clerical and monastic orders; for our suffering

Russian land and her Orthodox people both in the homeland and in the diaspora; for our brethren confined in prisons, and in bitter labours and in every affliction; for the peace and well-being of the whole world; for the well-being of the holy churches of God; for the salvation and help of our brethren who are labouring and serving with heedfulness and the fear of God; for the healing of them that lie in infirmities; for the repose, the release in blessed memory and remission of sins of all our fathers and brethren gone to their rest before us, and the Orthodox here and everywhere laid to rest; for the salvation of the people that stand here and pray, each of them calling to remembrance their transgressions; and in behalf of all and for all.

CHOIR: And in behalf of all and for all.

Priest (Bishop): And grant unto us that with one mouth and one heart we may glorify and hymn Thy most honourable and majestic name: of the Father, and of the Son, and of the Holy Spirit, now and ever, and unto the ages of ages.

CHOIR: Amen.

Priest (Bishop): And may the mercies of our great God and Saviour Jesus Christ be with you all.

CHOIR: And with thy spirit.

Deacon (Priest): Having called to remembrance all the saints, again and again, in peace let us pray to the Lord.

CHOIR: Lord, have mercy.

Deacon (Priest): For the precious Gifts offered and sanctified, let us pray to the Lord.

CHOIR: Lord, have mercy.

Deacon (Priest): That our God, the Lover of mankind, having accepted them upon His holy and most heavenly and noetic altar as an odour of spiritual fragrance, will send down upon us divine grace and the gift of the Holy Spirit, let us pray.

CHOIR: Lord, have mercy.

Deacon (Priest): That we may be delivered from all tribulation, wrath, and necessity, let us pray to the Lord.

CHOIR: Lord, have mercy. (*Slowly, if there be no deacon.*)

Deacon (Priest): Help us, save us, have mercy on us, and keep us, O God, by Thy grace.

CHOIR: Lord, have mercy.

Deacon (Priest): That the whole day may be perfect, holy, peaceful, and sinless, let us ask of the Lord.

CHOIR: Grant this, O Lord.

Deacon (Priest): An angel of peace, a faithful guide, a guardian of our souls and bodies, let us ask of the Lord.

CHOIR: Grant this, O Lord.

Deacon (Priest): Pardon and remission of our sins and offences, let us ask of the Lord.

CHOIR: Grant this, O Lord.

Deacon (Priest): Things good and profitable for our souls, and peace for the world, let us ask of the Lord.

CHOIR: Grant this, O Lord.

Deacon (Priest): That we may complete the remaining time of our life in peace and repentance, let us ask of the Lord.

CHOIR: Grant this, O Lord.

Deacon (Priest): A Christian ending to our life, painless, blameless, peaceful, and a good defence before the dread judgment seat of Christ, let us ask.

CHOIR: Grant this, O Lord.

Deacon (Priest): Having asked for the unity of the faith and the communion of the Holy Spirit, let us commit ourselves and one another and all our life unto Christ our God.

CHOIR: To Thee, O Lord.

Priest (Bishop): And vouchsafe us, O Master, that with boldness and without condemnation we may dare to call upon Thee the heavenly God as Father, and to say:

CHOIR (*and People*): Our Father, Who art in the heavens, * hallowed be Thy name. Thy kingdom come, * Thy will be done, on earth as it is in heaven. * Give us this day our daily bread; * and forgive us our debts, as we forgive our debtors; * and lead us not into temptation, * but deliver us from the evil one.

Priest (Bishop): For Thine is the kingdom, and the power, and the glory: of the Father, and of the Son, and of the Holy Spirit, now and ever, and unto the ages of ages.

CHOIR: Amen.

Priest (Bishop): Peace be unto all.

CHOIR: And to thy spirit.

Deacon (Priest): Bow your heads unto the Lord.

CHOIR: To Thee, O Lord. *(Slowly)*

Priest (Bishop): Through the grace and compassions and love for mankind of Thine Only-begotten Son, with Whom Thou art blessed, together with Thy Most-holy and good and life-creating Spirit, now and ever, and unto the ages of ages.

CHOIR: Amen. *(Slowly)*

Deacon (Priest): Let us attend!

Priest (Bishop): Holy Things are for the holy.

CHOIR: One is Holy, One is Lord, Jesus Christ, to the glory of God the Father. Amen.

And the communion verse of the day, or the saint, or the feast. For most Sundays it is: Praise the Lord from the heavens, praise Him in the highest. Alleluia, alleluia, alleluia.

The holy doors and curtain are closed while the priest taketh (clergy take) Communion. During this interval there may be chanting by the choir, or reading from the prayers before Holy Communion, or a sermon may be given.

THE COMMUNION OF THE PEOPLE

Deacon (Priest): With fear of God and with faith draw nigh.

CHOIR: Blessed is He that cometh in the name of the Lord. God is the Lord, and hath appeared unto us.

Priest (Bishop): I believe, O Lord, and I confess that Thou art truly the Christ, the Son of the living God, Who didst come into the world to save sinners of whom I am chief. Moreover, I believe that this is truly Thy most pure Body, and that this is truly Thine Own precious Blood. Wherefore, I pray Thee: Have mercy on me and forgive me my transgressions, voluntary and involuntary, in word and deed, in knowledge and in ignorance. And vouchsafe me to partake without condemnation of Thy most pure Mysteries unto the remission of sins and life everlasting.

Of Thy Mystical Supper, O Son of God, receive me today as a communicant; for I will not speak of the Mystery to Thine enemies, nor will I give Thee a kiss as did Judas, but like the Thief do I confess Thee: Remember me, O Lord, in Thy kingdom.

Let not the communion of Thy holy Mysteries be unto me for judgment or condemnation O Lord, but for healing of soul and body.

And to each communicant separately, the priest (bishop) saith:

The servant (*handmaid*) of God, *N.*, partaketh of the precious and holy Body and Blood of our Lord God and Saviour Jesus Christ, unto the remission of sins and life everlasting.

And as the people receive Holy Communion the choir chanteth, repeating until all have finished:

CHOIR: Receive ye the Body of Christ; taste ye of the Fountain of Immortality. And they conclude with: Alleluia, alleluia. alleluia.

Priest (Bishop): Save, O God, Thy people and bless Thine inheritance.

CHOIR: We have seen the True Light, we have received the Heavenly Spirit, we have found the True Faith, we worship the indivisible Trinity: for He hath saved us.

Priest: Always, now and ever, and unto the ages of ages.

CHOIR: Amen. Let our mouth be filled with Thy praise, O Lord, that we may hymn Thy glory, for Thou hast vouchsafed us to partake of Thy holy, divine, immortal, and life-giving Mysteries. Keep us in Thy holiness, that we may meditate on Thy righteousness all the day long. Alleluia, alleluia, alleluia.

Deacon (Priest): Aright! Having partaken of the divine, holy, most pure, immortal, heavenly, and life-giving, fearful Mysteries of Christ, let us worthily give thanks unto the Lord.

CHOIR: Lord, have mercy.

Deacon (Priest): Help us, save us, have mercy on us, and keep us, O God, by Thy grace.

CHOIR: Lord, have mercy.

Deacon (Priest): Having asked that the whole day may be perfect, holy, peaceful, and sinless, let us commit ourselves and one another and all our life unto Christ our God.

CHOIR: To Thee, O Lord.

Priest (Bishop): For Thou art our sanctification, and unto Thee do we send up glory: to the Father, and to the Son, and to the Holy Spirit, now and ever, and unto the ages of ages.

CHOIR: Amen.

Deacon (Priest): In peace let us depart.

CHOIR: In the name of the Lord.

Deacon (Priest): Let us pray to the Lord.

CHOIR: Lord, have mercy. (*Slowly, if there*

be no deacon.)

THE PRAYER BEHIND THE AMBO

Priest:

O Lord Who dost bless them that bless Thee and sanctify them that put their trust in Thee: Save Thy people and bless Thine inheritance; preserve the fullness of Thy Church, sanctify them that love the beauty of Thy house; do Thou glorify them by Thy divine power, and forsake us not that hope in Thee. Give peace to Thy world, to Thy churches, to the priests, and to all Thy people. For every good gift and every perfect gift is from above, and cometh down from Thee, the Father of lights, and unto Thee do we send up glory and thanksgiving and worship: to the Father, and to the Son, and to the Holy Spirit, now and ever, and unto the ages of ages.

CHOIR: Amen. Blessed be the name of the Lord from henceforth and for evermore. *Thrice.*

Priest (Bishop): The blessing of the Lord be upon you, through His grace and love for mankind, always, now and ever, and unto the ages of ages.

CHOIR: Amen.

Priest (Bishop): Glory to Thee, O Christ God, our hope, glory to Thee.

CHOIR: Glory to the Father, and to the Son, and to the Holy Spirit, both now and ever, and unto the ages of ages. Amen.

Lord, have mercy. *Thrice.*

Father (master), bless.

Priest (Bishop): May Christ our true God, (*On Sundays:* Who rose from the dead), through the intercessions of His most pure Mother, of the holy and glorious apostles, of our father among the saints, John Chrysostom, archbishop of Constantinople (*or* Basil the Great, archbishop of Caesarea in Cappadocia), and Saint(s) *N.(N.)* (*to whom the church is dedicated*), and Saint (s) *N.(N.)* (*commemorated on this date*), of the holy and righteous ancestors of God, Joachim and Anna, and of all the saints, have mercy on us and save us, for He is good and the Lover of mankind.

CHOIR: Amen. *And the Many Years:*

The Orthodox episcopate of the Church of Russia;* our lord the Very Most Reverend Metropolitan *N.*, First Hierarch of the Russian

Church Abroad,* and our lord the Most Reverend Archbishop (*or* Bishop) *N.*;* the brotherhood of this holy temple (*or* monastery), and all Orthodox Christians:* preserve, O Lord, for many years.

THE END OF THE DIVINE LITURGY

THE PRAYERS AFTER HOLY COMMUNION

When thou hast received the good Communion of the life-giving Mystical Gifts, give praise immediately, give thanks greatly, and from the soul say fervently unto God these things:

Glory to Thee, O God.
Glory to Thee, O God.
Glory to Thee, O God.

Then, this **Prayer of Thanksgiving, I***:*

I thank Thee, O Lord my God, that Thou hast not rejected me, a sinner, but hast vouchsafed me to be a communicant of Thy Holy Things. I thank Thee that Thou hast vouchsafed me, the unworthy, to partake of Thy most pure and heavenly Gifts. But, O Master, Lover of mankind, Who for our sake didst die and didst rise again, and didst bestow upon us these dread and life-giving Mysteries for the well-being and sanctification of our souls and bodies, grant that these may be even unto me for the healing of both soul and body, for the averting of everything hostile, for the enlightenment of the eyes of my heart, for the peace of the powers of my soul, for faith unashamed, for love unfeigned, for the fullness of wisdom, for the keeping of Thy commandments, for an increase of Thy divine grace, and for the attainment of Thy kingdom; that being preserved by them in Thy holiness, I may remember Thy grace always, and no longer live for myself, but for Thee, our Master and Benefactor; and thus when I shall have departed this life in hope of life eternal, I may attain unto everlasting rest, where the sound of them that keep festival is unceasing, and the delight is endless of them that behold the ineffable beauty of Thy countenance. For Thou art the true desire and the unutterable gladness of them that love Thee, O Christ our God, and all creation doth hymn Thee unto the ages. Amen.

Prayer II, of Basil the Great:

O Master Christ God, King of the ages and Creator of all things, I thank Thee for all the good things which Thou hast bestowed upon me, and for the communion of Thy most pure and life creating Mysteries. I pray Thee, therefore, O Good One and Lover of mankind: Keep me under Thy protection and in the shadow of Thy wings; and grant me, even until my last breath, to partake worthily, with a pure conscience, of Thy Holy Things, unto the remission of sins and life eternal. For Thou art the Bread of life, the Source of holiness, the Giver of good things; and unto Thee do we send up glory, together with the Father and the Holy Spirit, now and ever, and unto the ages of ages. Amen.

Prayer III, Verses of Metaphrastes:

O Thou Who givest me willingly Thy Flesh as food, Thou Who art fire that doth consume the unworthy, let me not be scorched, O my Creator. But rather, enter Thou into my members, into all my joints, my reins, my heart. Burn up the thorns of all my sins. Purify my soul, sanctify my thoughts. Strengthen my substance together with my bones. Enlighten my simple five senses. Nail down the whole of me with the fear of Thee. Ever protect, preserve, and keep me from every soul-corrupting deed and word. Purify, cleanse, and adorn me; make me comely, give me understanding, and enlighten me. Show me to be the dwelling-place of Thy Spirit alone, and no longer the habitation of sin; that from me as Thine abode through the entry of Communion, every evil-doer, every passion may flee as from fire. As intercessors I offer unto Thee all the saints, the commanders of the bodiless hosts, Thy Forerunner, the wise apostles, and further, Thine undefiled, pure Mother, whose entreaties do Thou accept, O my compassionate Christ, and make Thy servant a child of light. For Thou alone art our sanctification, O Good One, and the radiance of our souls, and unto Thee as God and Master, we all send up glory, as is meet, every day.

Another Prayer:

O Lord Jesus Christ our God, may Thy holy Body be unto me for life eternal, and Thy precious Blood for the remission of sins; and may this Eucharist be unto me for joy, health, and gladness. And at Thy dread Second Coming vouchsafe me, a sinner, to stand at the right hand of Thy glory, through the intercessions of Thy most pure Mother and of all the saints.

Another Prayer, to the Most Holy Theotokos:

O most holy Lady Theotokos, light of my darkened soul, my hope, protection, refuge, consolation, my joy: I thank thee that thou hast vouchsafed me, who am unworthy, to be a partaker of the most pure Body and precious Blood of thy Son. O thou who gavest birth to the True Light, do thou enlighten the spiritual eyes of my heart; thou who gavest birth to the Source of immortality, revive me who am dead in sin; thou who art the lovingly-compassionate Mother of the merciful God, have mercy on me, and grant me compunction and contrition in my heart, and humility in my thoughts, and the recall of my thoughts from captivity. And vouchsafe me, until my last breath, to receive without condemnation the sanctification of the most pure Mysteries, for the healing of both soul and body; and grant me tears of repentance and confession, that I may hymn and glorify thee all the days of my life, for blessed and most glorious art thou unto the ages. Amen.

Then: Now lettest Thou Thy servant depart in peace, O Master, according to Thy word; for mine eyes have seen Thy salvation, which Thou hast prepared before the face of all peoples, a light of revelation for the Gentiles, and the glory of Thy people Israel.

Holy God, Holy Mighty, Holy Immortal, have mercy on us. *Thrice.*

Glory to the Father, and to the Son, and to the Holy Spirit, both now and ever, and unto the ages of ages. Amen.

O Most Holy Trinity, have mercy on us. O Lord, blot out our sins. O Master, pardon our iniquities. O Holy One, visit and heal our infirmities for Thy name's sake.

Lord, have mercy. *Thrice.*

Glory to the Father, and to the Son, and to the Holy Spirit, both now and ever, and unto the ages of ages. Amen.

Our Father, Who art in the heavens, hallowed be Thy name. Thy kingdom come, Thy will be done, on earth as it is in heaven. Give us this day our daily bread, and forgive us our debts, as we forgive our debtors; and lead us not into temptation, but deliver us from the evil one.

If it be the Liturgy of St. John Chrysostom:

Grace shining forth from thy mouth like a beacon hath illumined the universe, and disclosed to the world treasures of uncovetousness, and shown us the heights of humility; but while instructing by thy words, O Father John Chrysostom, intercede with the Word, Christ our God, to save our souls.

Glory to the Father and to the Son, and to the Holy Spirit.

From the heavens hast thou received divine grace and by thy lips thou dost teach all to worship the One God in Trinity, O John Chrysostom, all-blessed righteous one. Rightly do we acclaim thee, for thou art a teacher revealing things divine.

But if it be the Liturgy of St. Basil the Great:

Thy fame hath gone forth into all the earth, which hath received thy word. Thereby thou hast divinely taught the Faith; thou hast made manifest the nature of created things; thou hast made the moral life of men a royal priesthood. O Basil, our righteous father, intercede with Christ God that our souls be saved.

Glory to the Father, and to the Son, and to the Holy Spirit.

Thou didst prove to be an unshakable foundation of the Church, giving to all mortals an inviolate lordship, and sealing it with thy doctrines, O righteous Basil, revealer of heavenly things.

Then: Both now and ever, and unto the ages of ages. Amen.

O protection of Christians that cannot be put to shame, O mediation unto the Creator unfailing, disdain not the suppliant voices of sinners; but be thou quick, O good one, to help us who in faith cry unto thee; hasten to intercession and speed thou to make supplication, thou who dost ever protect, O, Theotokos, them that honour thee.

Lord, have mercy. *Twelve times.*

Glory to the Father, and to the Son, and to the Holy Spirit, both now and ever, and unto the ages of ages. Amen.

More honorable than the Cherubim, and beyond compare more glorious than the Seraphim, who without corruption gavest birth to God the Word, the very Theotokos, thee do we magnify.

And the dismissal.

�֍✖✖✖✖✖✖

VARIABLE PORTIONS OF THE DIVINE LITURGY

TROPARIA, KONTAKIA, PROKEIMENA, AND COMMUNION VERSES

The Sunday Services from the Octoechos
FIRST TONE:

The Troparion of the Resurrection:

When the stone had been sealed by the Jews,* and the soldiers were guarding Thine immaculate Body,* Thou didst rise on the third day, O Saviour,* granting life unto the world.* Wherefore the hosts of the heavens cried out to Thee, O Life-giver:* Glory to Thy Resurrection, O Christ.* Glory to Thy kingdom.* Glory to Thy dispensation, O only Lover of mankind.

The Kontakion of the Resurrection:

As God Thou didst arise from the tomb in glory,* and Thou didst raise the world together with Thyself.* And mortal nature praiseth Thee as God,* and death hath vanished.* And Adam danceth, O Master,* and Eve now freed from fetters rejoiceth as she crieth out:* Thou art He, O Christ,* that grantest unto all resurrection.

Prokeimenon: Let Thy mercy, O Lord, be upon us, according as we have hoped in Thee. *(Psalm 32:22)*

Stichos: Rejoice in the Lord, O ye righteous; praise is meet for the upright. *(Ps.32:1)*

Alleluia: O God Who givest avengement unto me and hast subdued peoples under me. *(Ps.17:48)*

Stichos: It is He that magnifieth the salvation of His king and worketh mercy for His anointed, for David and for his seed unto eternity. *(Ps.17:51)*

Communion Verse *(for all Sundays except where otherwise indicated):* Praise the Lord from the heavens, praise Him in the highest.

SECOND TONE:

The Troparion of the Resurrection:

When Thou didst descend unto death, O Life Immortal, * then didst Thou slay hades with the lightning of Thy Divinity. * And when Thou didst also raise the dead out of the nethermost depths, * all the Hosts of the heavens cried out: * O Life-giver, Christ our God, glory be to Thee.

The Kontakion of the Resurrection:

Thou didst rise from the tomb, O omnipotent Saviour,* and hades was terrified on beholding the wonder;* and the dead arose,* and creation at the sight thereof rejoiceth with Thee.* And Adam also is joyful,* and the world, O my Saviour, praiseth Thee for ever.

Prokeimenon: The Lord is my strength and my song, and He is become my salvation. *(Ps.117:14)*

Stichos: With chastisement hath the Lord chastened me, but He hath not given me over unto death. *(Ps.117:18)*

Alleluia: The Lord hear thee in the day of affliction; the name of the God of Jacob defend thee. *(Ps.19:1)*

Stichos: O Lord, save the king, and hearken unto us in the day when we call upon Thee. *(Ps.19:9)*

THIRD TONE:

The Troparion of the Resurrection:

Let the heavens be glad; let earthly things rejoice;* for the Lord hath wrought might with His arm.* He hath trampled down death by death;* the first-born of the dead hath He become.* From the belly of hades hath He delivered us* and hath granted to the world great mercy.

The Kontakion of the Resurrection:

Thou didst rise today from the tomb, O Merciful One,* and didst lead us out of the gates of death.* Today Adam danceth and Eve rejoiceth;* and together with them both the prophets and patriarchs* unceasingly praise the divine might of Thine authority.

Prokeimenon: O chant unto our God, chant ye; chant unto our King, chant ye. *(Ps. 46:6)*

Stichos: Clap your hands, all ye nations; shout unto God with a voice of rejoicing. *(Ps. 46:1)*

Alleluia: In Thee, O Lord, have I hoped, let me not be put to shame in the age to come. *(Ps. 30:1)*

Stichos: Be Thou unto me a God to defend me and a house of refuge to save me. *(Ps. 30:2)*

FOURTH TONE:

The Troparion of the Resurrection:

Having learned the joyful proclamation of the Resurrection from the angel,* and having cast off the ancestral condemnation,* the women disciples of the Lord spake to the apostles exultantly:* Death is despoiled and Christ God is risen,* granting to the world great mercy.

The Kontakion of the Resurrection:

My Saviour and Redeemer hath, as God,* raised up the earthborn from the grave and from their fetters,* and He hath broken the gates of hades, *and, as Master,* hath risen on the third day.

Prokeimenon: How magnified are Thy works O Lord! In wisdom hast Thou made them all. *(Ps. 103:26)*

Stichos: Bless the Lord, O my soul; O Lord my God, Thou hast been magnified exceedingly. *(Ps.103:1)*

Alleluia: Bend Thy bow, and proceed prosperously, and be king, because of truth and meekness and righteousness. *(Ps.44:3)*

Stichos: Thou hast loved righteousness and hated iniquity. *(Ps.44:6)*

FIFTH TONE:

The Troparion of the Resurrection:

Let us, O faithful, praise and worship the Word* Who is co-unoriginate with the Father and the Spirit,* and Who was born of the Virgin for our salvation; * for He was pleased to ascend the Cross in the flesh * and to endure death, * and to raise the dead by His glorious Resurrection.

The Kontakion of the Resurrection:

Unto hades, O my Saviour, didst Thou descend, * and having broken its gates as one omnipotent, * Thou, as Creator, didst raise up the dead together with Thyself. * And Thou didst break the sting of death, * and didst deliver Adam from the curse, O Lover of mankind. * Wherefore, we all cry unto Thee: * Save us, O Lord.

Prokeimenon: Thou, O Lord, shalt keep us and shalt preserve us from this generation and for evermore. *(Ps.11:7)*

Stichos: Save me, O Lord, for a righteous man there is no more. *(Ps.11:1)*

Alleluia: Of Thy mercies, O Lord, will I sing for ever. Unto generation and generation will I declare Thy truth with my mouth. *(Ps.88:1,2)*

Stichos: For Thou hast said: Mercy shall be built up for ever, in the heavens shall Thy truth be established. *(Ps.88:3)*

SIXTH TONE:

The Troparion of the Resurrection:

Angelic hosts were above Thy tomb,* and they that guarded Thee became as dead.* And Mary stood by the grave seeking Thine immaculate Body.* Thou didst despoil hades and wast not tempted by it.* Thou didst meet the Virgin and didst grant us life.* O Thou Who didst rise from the dead, O Lord, glory be to Thee.

The Kontakion of the Resurrection:

Having by His life-bestowing hand raised up all the dead out of the dark abysses,* Christ God, the Giver of life, hath bestowed the Resurrection upon the fallen human race;* for He is the Saviour of all,* the Resurrection, and the Life, and the God of all.

Prokeimenon: Save, O Lord, Thy people and bless Thine inheritance. *(Psalm 27:9)*

Stichos: Unto Thee, O Lord, will I cry; O my God, be not silent unto me. *(Ps.27:1)*

Alleluia: He that dwelleth in the help of the Most High shall abide in the shelter of the God of heaven. *(Ps.90:1)*

Stichos: He shall say unto the Lord: Thou

art my helper and my refuge. He is my God, and I will hope in Him.

SEVENTH TONE:

The Troparion of the Resurrection:

Thou didst destroy death by Thy Cross, * Thou didst open paradise to the thief. * Thou didst change the lamentation of the Myrrh-bearers, * and Thou didst command Thine Apostles to proclaim *that Thou didst arise, O Christ God, * and grantest to the world great mercy.

The Kontakion of the Resurrection:

No longer will the dominion of death be able to keep men captive; * for Christ hath descended, demolishing and destroying the powers thereof. * Hades is bound; * the prophets rejoice with one voice, saying: * A Saviour hath come for them that have faith. * Come forth, ye faithful, for the Resurrection.

Prokeimenon: The Lord will give strength unto His people; the Lord will bless His people with peace. *(Ps.28:11)*

Stichos: Bring unto the Lord, ye sons of God, bring unto the Lord the sons of rams. *(Ps.28:1)*

Alleluia: It is good to give praise unto the Lord, and to chant unto Thy name, O Most High. *(Ps.92:1)*

Stichos: To proclaim in the morning Thy mercy, and Thy truth by night. *(Ps.91:2)*

EIGHTH TONE:

The Troparion of the Resurrection:

From on high didst Thou descend, O Compassionate One;* to burial of three days hast Thou submitted* that Thou mightest free us from our passions.* O our Life and Resurrection, O Lord, glory be to Thee.

The Kontakion of the Resurrection:

Having risen from the tomb, Thou didst raise up the dead. and didst resurrect Adam.* Eve also danceth at Thy Resurrection,* and the ends of the world celebrate Thine arising from the dead, O Greatly-merciful One.

Prokeimenon: Make your vows and pay them to the Lord our God. *(Ps.75:10)*

Stichos: In Judea is God known, His name is great in Israel. *(Ps.75:1)*

Alleluia: Come let us rejoice in the Lord, let us shout with jubilation unto God our

Saviour. *(Ps.94:1)*

Stichos: Let us come before His countenance with thanksgiving, and with psalms let us shout in jubilation unto Him. *(Ps.94:2)*

✳✳✳✳✳✳

THE WEEKDAY SERVICES FROM THE OCTOECHOS

MONDAY - The Bodiless Hosts.

Troparion, Fourth Tone: Supreme Commanders of the heavenly hosts, we unworthy ones implore you that by your supplications ye will encircle us with the shelter of the wings of your immaterial glory, and guard us who fall down before you and fervently cry: Deliver us from dangers since ye are the Marshalls of the Hosts on high.

Kontakion, Second Tone: Supreme Commanders of God and ministers of the Divine Glory, guides of men and leaders of the angels, ask for what is to our profit and for great mercy, since ye are the Supreme Commanders of the Bodiless Hosts.

Prokeimenon, Fourth Tone: Who maketh His angels spirits, and His ministers a flame of fire. *(Ps.103:5)*

Stichos: Bless the Lord, O my soul; O Lord my God, Thou hast been magnified exceedingly. *(Ps.103:1)*

Alleluia, Fifth Tone: Praise the Lord, all ye

His angels; praise Him, all ye His hosts.

Stichos: For He spake, and they came to be; He commanded and they were created.

Communion Verse: Who maketh His angels spirits, and His ministers a flame of fire.

TUESDAY - St. John the Forerunner.

Troparion, Second Tone: The memory of the righteous is celebrated with hymns of praise, but the Lord's testimony is sufficient for thee, O Forerunner; for thou hast proved to be truly even more venerable than the prophets, since thou wast granted to baptize in the running waters Him Whom they proclaimed. Wherefore, having contested for the truth, thou didst rejoice to announce the good tidings even to those in hades: that God hath appeared in the flesh, taking away the sin of the world and granting us great mercy.

Kontakion, Second Tone: O Prophet of God and Forerunner of grace, having obtained thy head from the earth as a most sacred rose, we ever receive healings; for again, as of old in the world, thou preachest repentance.

Prokeimenon, Seventh Tone: The righteous man shall be glad in the Lord, and shall hope in Him. *(Ps.63:11)*

Stichos: Hearken, O God, unto my prayer, when I make supplication unto Thee. *(Ps.63:1)*

Alleluia, Fourth Tone: The righteous man shall flourish like a palm tree, and like a cedar in Lebanon shall he be multiplied. *(Ps.91:11)*

Stichos: They that are planted in the house of the Lord, in the courts of our God they shall blossom forth. *(Ps.91:12)*

Communion Verse: In everlasting remembrance shall the righteous be, he shall not be afraid of evil tidings. *(Ps.111:6)*

WEDNESDAY - Troparion to the Cross

First Tone: Save, O Lord, Thy people, and bless Thine inheritance; grant Thou unto Orthodox Christians victory over enemies; and by the power of Thy Cross do Thou preserve Thy commonwealth.

Kontakion to the Cross, Fourth Tone: O Thou Who wast lifted up willingly on the Cross, bestow Thy mercies upon the new community named after Thee, O Christ God; gladden with Thy power the Orthodox Christians, granting them victory over enemies; may they have as Thy help the weapon of peace, the invincible trophy.

Prokeimenon, the Song of the Theotokos, Third Tone: My soul doth magnify the Lord, and my spirit hath rejoiced in God my Saviour. *(Luke 1:46,47)*

Stichos: For He hath looked upon the lowliness of His handmaiden; for behold, from henceforth all generations shall call me blessed.

Alleluia, Eighth Tone: Hearken, O daughter, and see, and incline thine ear. *(Ps.44:9)*

Stichos: The rich among the people shall entreat thy countenance. *(Ps.44:11)*

Communion Verse: I will take the cup of salvation, and I will call upon the name of the Lord. *(Ps.115:4)*

THURSDAY- The Holy Apostles and St. Nicholas.

Troparion to the Holy Apostles, Third Tone: O holy Apostles, intercede with the merciful God, that He grant unto our souls forgiveness of offences.

Troparion to St. Nicholas, Fourth Tone: The truth of things revealed thee to thy flock as rule of faith, an icon of meekness and a teacher of temperance; therefore thou hast achieved the heights by humility, riches by poverty. O Father and Hierarch Nicholas, intercede with Christ God that our souls be saved.

Kontakion to the Holy Apostles, Second Tone: The firm and divine-voiced preachers, the chief of Thy disciples, O Lord, Thou hast taken to Thyself for the enjoyment of Thy blessings and for repose; their labours and death didst Thou accept as above every sacrifice, O Thou Who alone knowest the hearts.

Kontakion to St. Nicholas, Third Tone:

In Myra, O Saint, thou didst prove to be a minister of things sacred; for having fulfilled the Gospel of Christ, O righteous one, thou didst lay down thy life for thy people, and didst save the innocent from death. Wherefore, thou wast sanctified, as a great initiate of the grace of God.

Prokeimenon, Eighth Tone: Their sound hath gone forth into all the earth, and their words unto the ends of the world. *(Ps. 18:4)*

Stichos: The heavens declare the glory of God, and the firmament proclaimeth the work of His hands. *(Ps.18:1)*

Alleluia, First Tone: The heavens shall confess Thy wonders, O Lord, and Thy truth in the congregation of saints. *(Ps.88:5)*

Stichos: God Who is glorified in the council of the saints. *(Ps.88:7)*

Communion Verse: Their sound hath gone forth into all the earth, and their words unto the ends of the world.

FRIDAY - Troparion to the Cross, First Tone:
Save, O Lord, Thy people, and bless Thine inheritance; grant Thou unto Orthodox Christians victory over enemies; and by the power of Thy Cross do Thou preserve Thy commonwealth.

Kontakion to the Cross, Fourth Tone:
O Thou Who wast lifted up willingly on the Cross, bestow Thy mercies upon the new community named after Thee, O Christ God; gladden with Thy power the Orthodox Christians, granting them victory over enemies; may they have as Thy help the weapon of peace, the invincible trophy.

Prokeimenon, Seventh Tone: Exalt ye the Lord our God and worship the footstool of His feet, for It is holy. *(Ps. 98:5)*

Stichos: The Lord is king, let the peoples rage. *(Ps. 98:1)*

Alleluia, First Tone: Remember Thy congregation which Thou hast purchased from the beginning. **(Ps. 73:2)**

Stichos: But God is our king before the ages, He hath wrought salvation in the midst of the earth. *(Ps. 73:11)*

Communion Verse: Thou hast wrought salvation in the midst of the earth, O God. *(Ps. 73:13)*

SATURDAY - All Saints and the Departed.
Troparion to All Saints, Second Tone:

O Apostles, Martyrs, and Prophets, Hierarchs, Monastics, and Righteous Ones; ye that have accomplished a good labour and kept the faith, that have boldness before the Saviour; O Good Ones, intercede for us, we pray, that our souls be saved.

Troparion for the Departed, Second Tone:

Remember, O Lord, Thy servants, for Thou art good, and forgive them whatsoever sins they have committed in life; for none is sinless but Thee, Who art able to give repose unto them that are departed.

If there be a saint's troparion, the preceding troparion is not said.

Kontakion for the Departed, Eighth Tone:

With the saints give rest, O Christ, to the souls of Thy servants, where there is neither sickness, nor sorrow, nor sighing, but life ever-lasting.

Kontakion to the Martyrs, Eighth Tone:

To Thee, O Lord, the Planter of creation, the world doth offer the God-bearing martyrs as the first-fruits of nature. By their intercessions preserve Thy Church, Thy common-wealth, in profound peace, through the Theotokos, O Greatly-merciful One.

Prokeimenon, Eighth Tone: Be glad in the Lord, and rejoice, ye righteous. *(Ps.31:11)*

Stichos: Blessed are they whose iniquities are forgiven, and whose sins are covered. *(31:1)*

Prokeimenon for the Departed, Sixth Tone: Their souls shall dwell among good things. *(Ps.24:13)*

Alleluia, Fourth Tone: The righteous cried, and the Lord heard them, and He delivered them out of all their tribulations. *(Ps.33:17)*

Stichos: Many are the tribulations of the

righteous, and the Lord shall deliver them out of them all. *(Ps.33:19)*

Stichos: Blessed are they whom Thou hast chosen and hast taken to Thyself, O Lord, and their memorial is unto generation and generation. *(Ps.64:4, and 134:13)*

Communion Verse: Rejoice in the Lord, O ye righteous; praise is meet for the upright.

Another: Blessed are they whom Thou hast chosen and hast taken to thyself, O Lord, and their memorial is unto generation and generation.

COMMON PROKEIMENA AND ALLELUIA OF SAINTS

TO THE MOST HOLY THEOTOKOS:

Prokeimenon, Third Tone: My soul doth magnify the Lord, and my spirit hath rejoiced in God my Saviour.

Stichos: For He hath looked upon the lowliness of His handmaiden; for behold, from henceforth all generations shall call me blessed.

Alleluia, Eighth Tone: Hearken, O daughter, and see, and incline thine ear. *(Ps.44:9)*

Stichos: The rich among the people shall entreat thy countenance. *(Ps.44:11)*

Communion Verse: I will take the cup of salvation, and I will call upon the name of the Lord. *(Ps.115:4)*

TO THE HEAVENLY BODILESS HOSTS:

Prokeimenon, Fourth Tone: Who maketh His angels spirits, and His ministers a flame of fire. *(Ps.103:5)*

Stichos: Bless the Lord, O my soul; O Lord my God, Thou hast been magnified exceedingly. *(Ps.103:1)*

Alleluia, Fifth Tone: Praise the Lord, all ye

His angels; praise Him all ye His hosts. *(148:2)*

Stichos: For He spake, and they came to be; He commanded, and they were created.

Communion Verse: Who maketh His angels spirits, and His ministers a flame of fire.

TO THE HOLY PROPHETS:

Prokeimenon, Fourth Tone: Thou art a priest for ever, after the order of Melchisedek.

Stichos: The Lord said unto my Lord: Sit Thou at My right hand, until I make Thine enemies the footstool of Thy feet. *(Ps.109:1)*

Alleluia, Fifth Tone: Moses and Aaron among His priests, and Samuel among them that call upon His name. *(Ps.98:6)*

Stichos: A light hath dawned forth for the righteous and gladness for the upright of heart. *(Ps.96:12)*

Communion Verse: In everlasting remembrance shall the righteous be, he shall not be afraid of evil tidings.

TO THE HOLY APOSTLES:

Prokeimenon, Eighth Tone: Their sound hath gone forth into all the earth, and their words unto the ends of the world. *(Ps.18:4)*

Stichos: The heavens declare the glory of

God and the firmament proclaimeth the work of His hands. *(Ps.18:1)*

Alleluia, First Tone: The heavens shall confess Thy wonders, O Lord, and Thy truth in the congregation of saints. *(Ps.88:5)*

Stichos: God Who is glorified in the council of the saints. *(Ps.88:7)*

Communion Verse: Their sound hath gone forth into all the earth, and their words unto the ends of the world.

TO A HIERARCH:

Prokeimenon, First Tone: My mouth shall speak wisdom, and the meditation of my heart shall be of understanding. *(Ps.48:3)*

Stichos: Hear this, all ye nations; give ear, all ye that inhabit the world.

Alleluia, Second Tone: The mouth of the righteous shall meditate wisdom and His tongue shall speak of judgment. *(Ps.36:31)*

Stichos: The law of God is in his heart, and his steps shall not be tripped. *(Ps.36:32)*

Communion Verse: In everlasting remembrance shall the righteous be; he shall not be afraid of evil tidings.

TO SEVERAL HIERARCHS:

Prokeimenon, Seventh Tone: Precious in the sight of the Lord is the death of His saints.

Stichos: What shall I render unto the Lord for all that he hath rendered unto me?

Alleluia, Second Tone: Thy priests shall be clothed with righteousness, and Thy righteous shall rejoice. *(Ps.131:9)*

Communion Verse: In everlasting remembrance shall the righteous be; he shall not be afraid of evil tidings.

TO MONK-SAINTS AND
FOOLS FOR THE SAKE OF CHRIST:

Prokeimenon, Seventh Tone: Precious in the sight of the Lord is the death of His saints.

Stichos: What shall I render unto the Lord for all that He hath rendered unto me?

Alleluia, Sixth Tone: Blessed is the man that feareth the Lord; in His commandments shall he greatly delight. *(Ps.111:1)*

Stichos: His seed shall be mighty upon the earth. *(Ps.111:2)*

Communion Verse: In everlasting remembrance shall the righteous be; he shall not be afraid of evil tidings.

TO A MARTYR:

Prokeimenon; Seventh Tone: The righteous man shall be glad in the Lord, and shall hope in Him. (Ps.63:11)

Stichos: Hearken, O God, unto my prayer, when I make supplication unto Thee. *(Ps.63:1)*

Alleluia, Fourth Tone: The righteous man shall flourish like a palm tree, and like a cedar in Lebanon shall he be multiplied. *(Ps.91:11)*

Stichos: They that are planted in the house of the Lord, in the courts of our God they shall blossom forth.

Communion Verse: In everlasting remembrance shall the righeous be; he shall not be afraid of evil tidings.

TO SEVERAL MARTYRS:

Prokeimenon, Fourth Tone: In the saints that are in His earth hath the Lord been wondrous; He hath wrought all His desires in them.

Stichos: I beheld the Lord ever before me, for He is at my right hand, that I might not be shaken. *(Ps.15:8)*

Alleluia Fourth Tone: The righteous cried, and the Lord heard them, and He delivered them out of all their tribulations. *(Ps.33:17)*

Stichos: Many are the tribulations of the righteous, and the Lord shall deliver them out of them all. *(Ps.33:19)*

Communion Verse: Rejoice in the Lord, O ye righteous; praise is meet for the upright.

TO A HIEROMARTYR:

Prokeimenon, Seventh Tone: The saints shall boast in glory, and they shall rejoice upon their beds. *(Ps.149:5)*

Stichos: Sing unto the Lord a new song; His praise is in the church of the saints.

Alleluia. Second Tone: Thy priests shall be clothed with righteousness, and Thy righteous shall rejoice. *(Ps.131:9)*

Communion Verse: In everlasting remembrance shall the righteous be; he shall not be afraid of evil tidings.

TO SEVERAL HIEROMARTYRS:

Prokeimenon, Seventh Tone: Precious in the sight of the Lord is the death of His saints.

Stichos: What shall I render unto the Lord for all that He hath rendered unto me.

Alleluia Second Tone: Thy priests shall be clothed with righteousness, and Thy righteous shall rejoice.

Communion Verse: Rejoice in the Lord, O ye righteous; praise is meet for the upright.

TO MONK-MARTYRS:

Prokeimenon, Seventh Tone: The saints shall boast in glory, and they shall rejoice upon their beds. *(Ps.149:5)*

Stichos: Sing unto the Lord a new song; His praise is in the church of the saints

Alleluia. Sixth Tone: Blessed is the man that feareth the Lord; in His commandments shall he greatly delight.

Stichos: His seed shall be mighty upon the earth.

Communion Verse: Rejoice in the Lord, O ye righteous; praise is meet for the upright.

TO HOLY WOMEN-MARTYRS:

Prokeimenon, Fourth Tone: Wondrous is God in His saints, the God of Israel.

Stichos: In congregations bless ye God, the Lord from the well-springs of Israel. *(Ps.67:27)*

Alleluia, First Tone: With patience I waited patiently for the Lord, and He was attentive unto me, and He hearkened unto my supplication. *(Ps.39:1)*

Communion Verse: Rejoice in the Lord, O

ye righteous; praise is meet for the upright.

TO NUN-SAINTS:

Prokeimenon, Fourth Tone: Wondrous is God in His saints, the God of Israel.

Stichos: In congregations bless ye God, the Lord from the well-springs of Israel. *(Ps.67:27)*

Alleluia, First Tone: With patience I waited patiently for the Lord, and He was attentive unto me, and He hearkened unto my supplication. *(Ps.39:1)*

Communion Verse: In everlasting remembrance shall the righteous be; he shall not be afraid of evil tidings.

TO CONFESSORS:

Prokeimenon, Seventh Tone: The saints shall boast in glory, and they shall rejoice upon their beds. *(Ps.149:5)*

Stichos: Sing unto the Lord a new song; His praise is in the church of the saints.

Alleluia. Sixth Tone: Blessed is the man that feareth the Lord; in His commandments shall he greatly delight.

Stichos: His seed shall be mighty upon the earth.

Communion Verse: Rejoice in the Lord, O

ye righteous; praise is meet for the upright.

TO UNMERCENARIES:

Prokeimenon, Fourth Tone: In the saints that are in His earth hath the Lord been wondrous; He hath wrought all His desires in them.

Stichos: I beheld the Lord ever before me, for He is at my right hand, that I might not be shaken. *(Ps.15:8)*

Alleluia, Second Tone: Behold now, what is so good or so joyous as for brethren to dwell together in unity? *(Ps.132:1)*

Communion Verse: Rejoice in the Lord O ye righteous; praise is meet for the upright.

FOR THE DEPARTED:

Prokeimenon, Sixth Tone: Their souls shall dwell among good things. *(Ps.24:13)*

Stichos: Unto Thee, O Lord, have I lifted up my soul. O my God, in Thee have I trusted; let me never be put to shame. *(Ps.24:1,2)*

Alleluia, Eighth Tone: Blessed are they whom Thou hast chosen and hast taken to Thyself, O Lord, and their memorial is unto generation and generation. *(Ps.64:4; 134:13)*

Communion Verse: Blessed are they whom

Thou hast chosen and hast taken to Thyself, O Lord, and their memorial is unto generation and generation.

❇❇❇❇❇❇

TROPARIA, KONTAKIA, AND PROKEIMENA FROM THE TRIODION

SUNDAY OF THE PUBLICAN AND THE PHARISEE:

Kontakion, Fourth Tone: Let us flee the bragging of the Pharisee, and learn the humility of the Publican, while crying out unto the Saviour with groanings: Be gracious unto us, O Thou Who alone dost readily forgive.

Another Kontakion, Third Tone: Unto the Lord let us sinners offer groanings like those of the Publican and let us fall down before Him, as He is Master. For He desireth the salvation of all men; He granteth forgiveness unto all that repent. For our sake He became incarnate, He Who with the Father is co-unoriginate God.

SUNDAY OF THE PRODIGAL SON:

Kontakion, Third Tone: Having foolishly abandoned Thy paternal glory, I squandered on vices the wealth which Thou gavest me. Wherefore, I cry unto Thee with the voice of the Prodigal: I have sinned before Thee, O compassionate Father. Receive me as one repentant, and make me as one of Thy hired servants.

MEAT-FARE SATURDAY:

Troparion, Eighth Tone: O Thou Who by the depth of Thy wisdom dost provide all things out of love for man, and grantest unto all that which is profitable, O only Creator: Grant rest, O Lord, to the souls of Thy servants; for in Thee have they placed their hope, O our Creator and Fashioner and God.

Glory, Kontakion, Eighth Tone: With the saints give rest, O Christ, to the souls of Thy servants, where there is neither sickness, nor sorrow, nor sighing, but life everlasting.

Both now, Theotokion: In thee we have a wall and a haven, and an intercessor acceptable to God Whom thou didst bear, O Theotokos unwedded, salvation of the faithful.

Prokeimenon, Sixth Tone: Their souls shall dwell among good things. *(Ps. 24:13)*

Stichos: Unto Thee, O Lord, have I lifted up my soul. O my God, in Thee have I trusted; let me never be put to shame. *(Ps. 24:2)*

Alleluia, Sixth Tone: Blessed are they whom Thou hast chosen and hast taken to

Thyself O Lord, and their memorial is unto generation and generation. *(Ps.64:4; 134:13)*

Stichos: Their souls shall dwell among good things.

Communion Verse: Blessed are they whom Thou hast chosen hast taken to Thyself, O Lord, and their memorial is unto generation and generation.

MEAT-FARE SUNDAY:

Kontakion, First Tone: When Thou, O God, shalt come to earth with glory, and all things tremble, and the river of fire floweth before the Judgment Seat and the books are opened, and the hidden things made public, then deliver me from the unquenchable fire and deem me worthy to stand at Thy right hand, O most righteous Judge.

Prokeimenon, Third Tone: Great is our Lord, and great is His strength, and of His understanding there is no measure.

Stichos: Praise ye the Lord, for a psalm is a good thing.

Alleluia, Eighth Tone: Come let us rejoice in the Lord, let us shout with jubilation unto God our Saviour. *(Ps.94:1)*

Stichos: Let us come before His countenance with thanksgiving, and with psalms let us shout in jubilation unto Him. *(Ps. 94:2)*

Communion Verse: Praise the Lord from the heavens, praise Him in the highest.

Another: Rejoice in the Lord, O ye righteous; praise is meet for the upright.

CHEESE-FARE SATURDAY:

Troparion, Fourth Tone: O God of our fathers, Who ever dealest with us according to Thy kindness, take not Thy mercy from us, but through their intercessions guide our life in peace.

Kontakion, Eighth Tone: Thou hast made the assembly of the God-bearers illustrious as preachers of piety and silencers of ungodliness, O Lord, and they shine upon the world. By their supplications, keep in perfect peace them that glorify and magnify Thee, that they may chant and sing unto Thee: Alleluia.

Prokeimenon, Fourth Tone: The saints shall boast in glory, and they shall rejoice upon their beds. *(Ps. 149:5)*

Stichos: The high praise of God shall be in their throat, and two-edged swords shall be in their hands.

Alleluia Second Tone: They that are planted in the house of the Lord, in the courts of our God they shall blossom forth. *(Ps.91:12)*

Stichos: The righteous man shall be glad in the Lord, and shall hope in Him. *(Ps.63:11)*

Communion Verse: Rejoice in the Lord, O ye righteous; praise is meet for the upright.

CHEESE-FARE SUNDAY:

Kontakion, Sixth Tone: O Thou guide unto wisdom, bestower of prudence, instructor of the foolish and defender of the poor: Establish and grant understanding unto my heart, O Master. Grant me speech, O Word of the Father; for behold, I shall not keep my lips from crying unto Thee: O Merciful One, have mercy on me who have fallen.

Prokeimenon, Eighth Tone: Make your vows and pay them to the Lord our God.

Stichos: In Judea is God known, His name is great in Israel. *(Ps.75:1)*

Alleluia, Sixth Tone: It is good to give praise unto the Lord, and to chant unto Thy name, O Most High. *(Ps.91:1)*

Stichos: To proclaim in the morning Thy

mercy, and Thy truth by night. *(Ps.91:2)*

Communion Verse: Praise the Lord from the heavens, praise Him in the highest.

THE FIRST SATURDAY OF GREAT LENT:
St. Theodore the Tyro

Troparion, Second Tone: Great are the achievements of faith! In the fountain of flame as in refreshing water, the holy martyr Theodore rejoiced; for having been made a whole-burnt offering in the fire, he was offered as sweet bread unto the Trinity. By his prayers, O Christ God, save our souls.

Kontakion, Eighth Tone: Having received the Faith of Christ in thy heart as a breastplate, thou didst trample upon the enemy hosts, O great champion; and thou hast been crowned eternally with a heavenly crown, as thou art invincible.

Prokeimenon, Seventh Tone: The righteous man shall be glad in the Lord, and shall hope in Him. *(Ps.63:11)*

Stichos: Hearken, O God, unto my prayer when I make supplication unto Thee. *(Ps.63:1)*

Alleluia Fourth Tone: The righteous man shall flourish like a palm tree, and like a cedar in Lebanon shall he be multiplied. *(Ps. 91:11)*

Stichos: They that are planted in the house of the Lord, in the courts of our God they shall blossom forth.

Communion Verse: In everlasting remembrance shall the righteous be; he shall not be afraid of evil tidings.

THE FIRST SUNDAY OF GREAT LENT:
The Triumph of Orthodoxy

Troparion, Second Tone: We worship Thine immaculate Icon, O Good One, asking the forgiveness of our failings, O Christ God; for of Thine Own will Thou wast well-pleased to ascend the Cross in the flesh that Thou mightest deliver from slavery to the enemy those whom Thou hadst fashioned. Wherefore, we cry to Thee thankfully: Thou didst fill all things with joy, O our Saviour, when Thou camest to save the world.

Kontakion, Eighth Tone: The uncircumscribable Word of the Father was circumscribed when He took flesh of thee, O Theotokos; and when He had restored the defiled image to its ancient state, He suffused it with divine beauty. As for us, confessing our salvation, we record it in deed and word.

Prokeimenon, Fourth Tone: the Song of the Fathers: Blessed art Thou, O Lord, the God of our fathers, and praised and glorified is Thy name unto the ages. *(Daniel 3:26)*

Stichos: For righteous art Thou in all which Thou hast done for us. *(Dan.3:27)*

Alleluia, Fourth Tone: Moses and Aaron among His priests, and Samuel among them that call upon His name.

Stichos: They called upon the Lord, and He hearkened unto them. *(Ps.98:7)*

Communion Verse: Praise the Lord from the heavens, praise Him in the highest.

Another: Rejoice in the Lord, O ye righteous; praise is meet for the upright.

THE SECOND SATURDAY OF LENT:

O Apostles, Martyrs, and Prophets,... Remember, O Lord, Thy servants,... **Glory:** With the Saints,... **Both now:** In thee we have a wall and a haven, and an intercessor acceptable to God Whom thou didst bear, O Theotokos unwedded, salvation of the faithful. *The prokeimenon, alleluia, and communion verse for Saturdays, and for the departed, page 127.*

THE SECOND SUNDAY OF GREAT LENT:
St. Gregory Palamas

Troparion, Eighth Tone: Light of Orthodoxy, pillar and teacher of the Church, adornment of monastics, invincible champion of theologians, O Gregory, thou wonderworker, boast of Thessalonica, herald of grace, ever pray that our souls be saved

Kontakion to St. Gregory, Eighth Tone:

O sacred and divine organ of wisdom, clear trumpet of theology: we praise thee with one accord, O Gregory of divine speech; but as a mind standing before the Primordial Mind, direct our mind to Him, O father, that we may cry: Rejoice, O herald of grace!

Kontakion of the Sunday, Fourth Tone:

The season of the virtues hath now been revealed, and judgment is at the doors; therefore let us arise and keep the Fast, offering tears of compunction together with our alms, and let us cry: Our sins are more than the sands of the sea; but do Thou pardon us, O Creator of all, that we may receive incorruptible crowns.

Prokeimenon, Fifth Tone: Thou, O Lord,

shalt keep us and shalt preserve us from this generation, and for evermore.

Stichos: Save me, O Lord, for a righteous man there is no more. *(Ps.11:1)*

For St. Gregory, Prokeimenon, First Tone: My mouth shall speak wisdom, and the meditation of my heart shall be of understanding.

Alleluia, Fifth Tone: Of Thy mercies, O Lord, will I sing for ever. Unto generation and generation will I declare Thy truth with my mouth.

Stichos: For Thou hast said: Mercy shall be built up for ever. In the heavens shall Thy truth be established.

Communion Verse: Praise the Lord from the heavens, praise Him in the highest.

Another: In everlasting remembrance shall the righteous be; he shall not be afraid of evil tidings.

THE THIRD SATURDAY OF GREAT LENT:

Everything same as for Second Saturday.

THE THIRD SUNDAY OF GREAT LENT:
Veneration of the Cross

Troparion, First Tone: Save, O Lord, Thy people and bless Thine inheritance; grant

Thou unto Orthodox Christians victory over enemies; and by the power of Thy Cross do Thou preserve Thy commonwealth.

Kontakion, Fourth Tone: O Thou Who wast lifted up willingly on the cross, bestow Thy mercies upon the new community named after Thee, O Christ God; gladden with Thy power the Orthodox Christians, granting them victory over enemies; may they have as Thy help the weapon of peace, the invincible trophy.

Another Kontakion, Seventh Tone:

No longer doth the flaming sword guard the gate of Eden, for a strange extinction hath come upon it, even the Tree of the Cross. The sting hath been taken from death, and the victory from hades. And Thou, my Saviour, didst appear unto those in hades, saying: Enter ye again into Paradise.

Instead of the Trisagion: Before Thy Cross we bow down, O Master, and Thy holy Resurrection we glorify.

Prokeimenon, Sixth Tone: Save, O Lord, Thy people and bless Thine inheritance.

Stichos: Unto Thee, O Lord, will I cry; O

my God, be not silent unto me. *(Ps.27:1)*

Alleluia, Eighth Tone: Remember Thy congregation which Thou hast purchased from the beginning. *(Ps.73:2)*

Stichos: But God is our king before the ages, He hath wrought salvation in the midst of the earth. *(Ps.73:13)*

Communion Verse: The light of Thy countenance, O Lord, hath been signed upon us.

THE FOURTH SATURDAY OF LENT:
Everything same as for the Second Saturday.
THE FOURTH SUNDAY OF GREAT LENT:
St. John of the Ladder

Troparion, Third Tone: Having raised up a sacred ladder by thy words, thou wast shown forth unto all as a teacher of monastics, and thou dost lead us, John, from the purification that cometh through godly discipline, unto the light of divine vision. O righteous Father, do thou entreat Christ God that we be granted great mercy.

Kontakion, First Tone: Offering teachings from thy book as ever-blossoming fruits, O wise one, thou dost sweeten the heart of them that attend to them with vigilance, O blessed one; for it is a ladder that, from earth unto the heavenly and abiding glory, doth lead the souls of those who with faith do honour thee.

Prokeimenon of the tone; and of the saint, Seventh Tone: The saints shall boast in glory, and they shall rejoice upon their beds.

Alleluia of the tone; and of the saint, Fourth Tone: They that are planted in the house of the Lord, in the courts of our God they shall blossom forth.

Communion Verse: Praise the Lord from the heavens, praise Him in the highest.

Another: In everlasting remembrance shall the righteous be; he shall not be afraid of evil tidings.

THE FIFTH SATURDAY OF GREAT LENT:
The Laudation of the Theotokos

Troparion, Eighth Tone: When the bodiless one learned the secret command, in haste he came and stood before Joseph's dwelling and spake unto the Maiden who knew not wedlock: The One who hath bowed the heavens by His descent is held and contained, unchanging, wholly in thee. Seeing Him receiving the form of a servant in thy womb, I stand in awe and cry to thee: Rejoice, thou Bride Unwedded.

Kontakion, Eighth Tone: To thee, the champion leader, we thy servants dedicate a feast of victory and of thanksgiving, as ones rescued out of sufferings, O Theotokos; but as thou art one with might which is invincible, from all dangers that can be do thou deliver us, that we may cry to thee: Rejoice, thou Bride Unwedded.

Prokeimenon, Third Tone, the Song of the Theotokos: My soul doth magnify the Lord, and my spirit hath rejoiced in God my Saviour.

Stichos: For He hath looked upon the lowliness of His handmaiden; for behold, from henceforth all generations shall call me blessed.

Alleluia, Eighth Tone: Arise, O Lord, into Thy rest, Thou and the ark of Thy holiness.

Stichos: Remember, O Lord, David and all his meekness.

Communion Verse: I will take the cup of salvation, and I will call upon the name of the Lord.

THE FIFTH SUNDAY OF GREAT LENT:
St. Mary of Egypt

Troparion, Fifth Tone: Enlightened by the grace of the cross, thou wast shown forth as a radiant lamp of repentance, dispelling the darkness of the passions, O all-holy one. Wherefore, thou didst appear as an angel in the flesh unto the sacred Zosimas in the wilderness. O Mary, our righteous mother, do thou intercede with Christ for us.

Kontakion, Third Tone: Thou who once of old wast filled with all manner of fornication, art now seen today to be a bride of Christ by thy repentance. Thou didst love and emulate the life of the angels. By the Cross thou didst annihilate the hordes of demons; for this cause thou art a bride now in the kingdom of the heavens, O Mary, thou all-modest one.

Another Kontakion, Fourth Tone: Having escaped the darkness of sin, and having illumined thy heart with the light of repentance, O glorious one, thou didst come to Christ and didst offer to Him His immaculate and holy Mother as a merciful intercessor. Hence thou hast found remission of thy transgressions, and thou ever rejoicest with the angels.

**Prokeimenon of the tone, and of the saint,

Fourth Tone: Wondrous is God in His saints, the God of Israel.

Alleluia of the tone.

Communion Verse: Praise the Lord from the heavens,.... **Another:** In everlasting remembrance shall the righteous be,....

THE SIXTH SATURDAY OF GREAT LENT:
Lazarus Saturday

Troparion, First Tone: In confirming the common Resurrection, O Christ God, Thou didst raise up Lazarus from the dead before Thy Passion. Wherefore, we also, like the children bearing the symbols of victory, cry to thee the Vanquisher of death: Hosanna in the highest; blessed is He that cometh in the name of the Lord.

Kontakion, Second Tone: Christ, the Joy of all, the Truth, the Light, the Life, the Resurrection of the world, hath, of His goodness, appeared to those on earth, and become the archetype of the Resurrection, granting divine forgiveness unto all.

Instead of the Trisagion: As many as have been baptized into Christ have put on Christ. Alleluia.

Prokeimenon, Third Tone: The Lord is my light and my saviour; whom then shall I fear?

Stichos: The Lord is the defender of my life; of whom then shall I be afraid? *(Ps. 26:1)*

Alleluia, Fifth Tone: The Lord is King, He is clothed with majesty. *(Ps. 92:1)*

Stichos: For He established the world which shall not be shaken. *(Ps. 92:2)*

Communion Verse: Out of the mouths of babes and sucklings hast Thou perfected praise. *(Ps. 8:2)*

PALM SUNDAY

THE FIRST ANTIPHON, Psalm 114, Second Tone:

Stichos 1: I am filled with love, for the Lord will hear the voice of my supplication.

Refrain: Through the prayers of the Theotokos, O Saviour, save us.

Stichos 2: For He hath inclined His ear unto me, and in my days will I call upon Him. *Refrain.*

Stichos 3: The pangs of death have encompassed me, the perils of hades have found me. *Refrain.*

Stichos 4: Tribulation and sorrow have I found, and I called upon the name of the Lord. *Refrain.*

Glory to the Father, and to the Son, and to the Holy Spirit, both now and ever, and unto the ages of ages. Amen. *Refrain.*

THE SECOND ANTIPHON, Psalm 115, Second Tone:

Stichos 1: I believed, wherefore I spake; I was humbled exceedingly.

Refrain: O Son of God, Who didst sit upon a colt, save us who chant unto Thee: Alleluia.

Stichos 2: What shall I render unto the Lord for all that He hath rendered unto me? *Refrain.*

Stichos 3: I will take the cup of salvation, and I will call upon the name of the Lord. *Refrain.*

Stichos 4: My vows unto the Lord will I pay in the presence of all His people. *Refrain.*

Glory to the Father, and to the Son, and to the Holy Spirit, both now and ever, and unto the ages of ages. Amen.

O Only-begotten Son and Word of God, Who art immortal....

THE THIRD ANTIPHON, Psalm 117, First Tone:

Stichos 1 (*Reader*): O give thanks unto the Lord, for He is good, for His mercy endureth for ever.

CHOIR, **Troparion, First Tone:**

In confirming the common Resurrection, O Christ God, Thou didst raise up Lazarus from the dead before Thy Passion. Wherefore, we also, like the children bearing the symbols of victory, cry to Thee, the Vanquisher of death: Hosanna in the highest; blessed is He that cometh in the name of the Lord.

Stichos 2: Let the house of Israel now say that He is good, for His mercy endureth for ever. *Troparion.*

Stichos 3: Let the house of Aaron now say that He is good, for His mercy endureth for ever. *Troparion.*

Stichos 4: Let all that fear the Lord now say that He is good, for His mercy endureth for ever. *Troparion.*

At the Small Entry, the Verse (said by the deacon or priest): Blessed is he that cometh in the name of the Lord. We have blessed you out of the house of the Lord. God is the Lord, and hath appeared unto us. *(Ps. 117:25, 26)*

CHOIR, the Troparion: In confirming the common Resurrection... *(see above)*.

Glory to the Father, and to the Son, and to the Holy Spirit.

Another Troparion, Fourth Tone: As by baptism we were buried with Thee, O Christ our God, so by Thy Resurrection we were deemed worthy of immortal life; and praising Thee, we cry: Hosanna in the highest; blessed is He that cometh in the name of the Lord.

Both now and ever, and unto the ages of ages. Amen.

Kontakion, Sixth Tone:

Being borne upon a throne in heaven, and upon a colt on the earth, O Christ God, Thou didst accept the praise of the angels and the laudation of the children as they cry to Thee: Blessed is He that cometh to recall Adam.

Prokeimenon, Fourth Tone: Blessed is he that cometh in the name of the Lord. God is the Lord, and hath appeared unto us.

Stichos: O give thanks unto the Lord, for He is good, for His mercy endureth for ever.

Alleluia, First Tone: O sing unto the Lord a new song, for the Lord hath wrought wondrous things. *(Ps. 97:1)*

Stichos: All the ends of the earth have seen the salvation of our God. *(Ps. 97:5)*

Instead of It is truly meet *we chant the Eirmos of the 9th Ode of the canon of the feast, Fourth Tone:*

God is the Lord, and hath appeared unto us; make ye a feast, and with gladness, come, let us magnify Christ with palms and branches, with hymns crying aloud: Blessed is He that cometh in the name of the Lord our Saviour.

Communion Verse: Blessed is he that cometh in the name of the Lord. God is the Lord, and hath appeared unto us.

ON HOLY AND GREAT THURSDAY:

The Prokeimenon, Seventh Tone: The rulers were assembled together, against the Lord, and against His Christ. *(Ps. 2:2)*

Stichos: Why have the heathen raged, and the peoples meditated empty things? *(Ps. 2:1)*

Alleluia, Sixth Tone: Blessed is the man that hath understanding for the poor man and the pauper; in an evil day the Lord will deliver him. *(Ps. 40:1)*

Stichos: Mine enemies have spoken evil things against me: When shall he die, and when shall his name perish? *(Ps. 40:5)*

Stichos: Who ate of my bread hath magnified the lifting of heels against me. *(Ps. 40:9)*

Instead of the Cherubic Hymn, we chant this Troparion, in the Sixth Tone, thrice: Of Thy Mystical Supper, O Son of God, receive me today as a communicant; for I will not speak of the Mystery to Thine enemies; nor will I give Thee a kiss, as did Judas, but like the thief do I confess Thee: Remember me, O Lord, in Thy kingdom.

Likewise we chant this as the Communion Verse, and also during the communion of the people instead of Receive ye the Body of Christ. *Also instead of* Let our mouth be filled with Thy praise....

ON HOLY AND GREAT SATURDAY:

Instead of the Trisagion: As many as have been baptized into Christ have put on Christ. Alleluia.

Prokeimenon, Fifth Tone: Let all the earth worship Thee and chant into Thee; let them chant unto Thy name, O Most High. *(Ps. 65:3)*

Stichos: Shout with jubilation unto the Lord all the earth; chant ye unto His name, give glory in praise of Him. *(Ps.65:1)*

Instead of Alleluia, the Reader saith: In the Seventh Tone: Arise, O God judge the earth for thou shalt have an inheritance among all the nations. *(Ps.81)*

CHOIR: Arise, O God, judge the earth, for Thou shalt have an inheritance among all the nations.

Reader, **Stichos:** God stood in the congregation of the gods, and in the midst He shall stand out among gods.

CHOIR: Arise, O God, judge the earth....

Stichos: How long will ye judge unrighteously and accept the person of sinners? *Refrain.*

Stichos: Judge for the orphan and the poor man, do justice to the humble and the pauper. *Refrain.*

Stichos: Rescue the poor man and the needy, from the hand of the sinner deliver him. *Refrain.*

Stichos: They have not known, nor understood; they walk in darkness. *Refrain.*

Stichos: Let all the foundations of the earth

be shaken. I said: ye are gods, and all of you the sons of the Most High. But like men ye die, and like one of the rulers do ye fall. *Refrain.*

And again the Reader: Arise, O God, judge the earth, for Thou shalt have an inheritance among all the nations.

Instead of the Cherubic Hymn, we chant the Troparion, Eighth Tone:

Let all mortal flesh keep silence, and stand with fear and trembling; and let it take no thought for any earthly thing. For the King of kings and Lord of lords draweth nigh to be sacrificed and given as food to the faithful. *(Here the Great Entry occurreth.)* Before Him go the choirs of angels with all the principalities and powers, the many-eyed cherubim and the six-winged seraphim, covering their faces and crying aloud the hymn: Alleluia, alleluia, alleluia.

Instead of It is truly meet *we chant the Eirmos of the 9th Ode of the Matins canon, Sixth Tone:* Weep not for Me, O Mother, beholding in the tomb the Son Whom thou hast conceived without seed in thy womb. For I shall arise and be glorified, and as God I shall exalt with glory unceasingly those that with faith and love magnify thee.

Communion Verse: The Lord awoke as one that sleepeth, and is risen, saving us. Alleluia. *(Ps. 77:70)*

THE END OF THE TRIODION

❋❋❋❋❋❋❋❋

THE HOLY AND GREAT
SUNDAY OF PASCHA

THE ORDER OF THE PASCHAL LITURGY

Deacon: Bless, master!

Priest: Blessed is the kingdom....

CHOIR: Amen. *And the clergy chant:*

Christ is risen from the dead, trampling down death by death, and on those in the tombs bestowing life. *Thrice. And the choir, thrice.*

And the celebrant saith the stichoi:

Stichos 1: Let God arise and let His enemies be scattered, and let them that hate Him flee from before His face.

And after each stichos the choir chanteth the Troparion: Christ is risen from the dead, trampling down death by death, and on those in the tombs bestowing life. *Once.*

Stichos 2: As smoke vanisheth, so let them vanish, as wax melteth before the fire.

CHOIR: Christ is risen....

Stichos 3: So let sinners perish at the presence of God, and let the righteous be glad.

CHOIR: Christ is risen....

Stichos 4: This is the day which the Lord

hath made; let us rejoice and be glad therein.

CHOIR: Christ is risen ....

Celebrant: Glory to the Father, and to the Son, and to the Holy Spirit.

CHOIR: Christ is risen....

Celebrant: Both now and ever, and unto the ages of ages. Amen.

CHOIR: Christ is risen ....

Clergy: Christ is risen from the dead, trampling down death by death. *CHOIR:* And on those in the tombs bestowing life.

THE FIRST ANTIPHON, Psalm 65, Second Tone:

Stichos 1: Shout with jubilation unto the Lord all the earth; chant ye unto His name, give glory in praise of Him.

Refrain: Through the prayers of the Theotokos, O Saviour, save us.

Stichos 2: Say unto God: How awesome are Thy works! In the multitude of Thy power shall Thine enemies be proved false unto Thee. *Refrain.*

Stichos 3: Let all the earth worship Thee and chant unto Thee; Let them chant unto Thy name, O Most High. *Refrain.*

Glory to the Father, and to the Son, and to the Holy Spirit, both now and ever, and unto the ages of ages. Amen. *Refrain.*

THE SECOND ANTIPHON, Psalm 66, Second Tone:

Stichos 1: God be gracious unto us and bless us, and cause Thy face to shine upon us and have mercy on us.

Refrain: O Son of God Who didst rise from the dead, save us who chant unto Thee: Alleluia.

Stichos 2: That we may know upon the earth Thy way, among all the nations Thy salvation. *Refrain.*

Stichos 3: Let all the peoples give Thee praise, O God, let all the peoples praise Thee. *Refrain.*

Glory to the Father, and to the Son, and to the Holy Spirit, both now and ever, and unto the ages of ages. Amen.

O Only-begotten Son and Word of God, Who art immortal....

THE THIRD ANTIPHON, Psalm 67, Fifth Tone:

Stichos 1 *(Reader)*: Let God arise and let

His enemies be scattered, and let them that hate Him flee from before His face.

CHOIR, the **Paschal Troparion:** Christ is risen from the dead, trampling down death by death, and on those in the tombs bestowing life. *Once (after each stichos).*

Stichos 2: As smoke vanisheth, so let them vanish, as wax melteth before the fire. *Troparion.*

Stichos 3: So let sinners perish at the presence of God, and let the righteous be glad, let them rejoice in the presence of God. *Troparion.*

At the Small Entry, the Verse (said by the deacon or priest): In congregations bless ye God, the Lord from the well-springs of Israel.

CHOIR, the **Paschal Troparion***:* Christ is risen from the dead, trampling down death by death, and on those in the tombs bestowing life.

And the Hypakoe, Eighth Tone:

Forestalling the dawn, the women came with Mary,* and found the stone rolled away from the sepulchre, and heard from the angel:* Why seek ye among the dead, as though He were mortal, Him Who liveth in everlasting light?* Behold the grave-clothes.

Go quickly and proclaim to the world that the Lord is risen and hath slain death.* For He is the Son of God Who saveth mankind.

And the Kontakion, same Tone:

Though Thou didst descend into the grave, O Immortal One,* yet didst Thou destroy the power of hades.* And didst arise as victor, O Christ God,* calling to the myrrh-bearing women: Rejoice!* and giving peace unto Thine apostles:* Thou Who dost grant resurrection to the fallen.

Instead of the Trisagion: As many as have been baptized into Christ have put on Christ. Alleluia. *Thrice.*

Glory to the Father, and to the Son, and to the Holy Spirit, both now and ever, and unto the ages of ages. Amen. Have put on Christ. Alleluia.

As many as have been baptized into Christ have put on Christ. Alleluia.

Prokeimenon, Eighth Tone: This is the day which the Lord hath made; let us rejoice and be glad therein.

Stichos: O give thanks unto the Lord, for He is good, for His mercy endureth for ever.

Alleluia, Fourth Tone: Thou shalt rise up and have pity upon Sion. *(Ps.101:13)*

Stichos: The Lord from heaven hath looked upon the earth. *(Ps.101:19)*

Instead of It is truly meet *we chant the Eirmos of 9th Ode, First Tone:*

Refrain: The angel cried unto her that is full of grace: O pure Virgin, rejoice! and again I say, rejoice! for thy Son is risen from the grave on the third day, and hath raised the dead, O ye people, be joyful!

Eirmos: Shine, shine, O new Jerusalem, for the glory the Lord is risen upon thee; dance now and be glad, O Sion, and do thou exult, O pure Theotokos, in the arising of Him Whom thou didst bear.

Communion Verse: Receive ye the Body of Christ, taste ye of the Fountain of Immortality. Alleluia, alleluia, alleluia.

When the celebrant saith With fear of God and with faith draw nigh, *instead of* Blessed is He that cometh in the name of the Lord *we chant:* Christ is risen from the dead, trampling down death by death, and on those in the tombs bestowing life. *Once.*

And when the celebrant saith Save, O God, Thy people, *we chant:* Christ is risen from the dead... *Once.*

And when he saith Always, now and ever, and unto the ages of ages, *we chant* Christ is risen from the dead... *Once.*

And instead of Blessed be the name of the Lord..., *we chant:* Christ is risen from the dead..., *twelve times, and more, until the celebrant has distributed the antidoron.*

Then the celebrant saith: The blessing of the Lord be upon you... *CHOIR:* Amen. *Then the clergy chant:* Christ is risen from the dead, trampling down death by death. *And the CHOIR:* And on those in the tombs bestowing life.

After this the celebrant saith the usual Dismissal and CHRIST IS RISEN, *thrice, while bestowing a blessing with the Cross.*

ON MONDAY OF BRIGHT WEEK:

Prokeimenon, Eighth Tone: Their sound hath gone forth into all the earth, and their words unto the ends of the world.

Stichos: The heavens declare the glory of God, and the firmament proclaimeth the work of His hands.

Alleluia, First Tone: The heavens shall confess Thy wonders, O Lord.

Stichos: God Who is glorified in the council of the saints.

Communion Verse: Receive ye the Body of Christ, taste ye of the Fountain of Immortality.

ON TUESDAY OF BRIGHT WEEK:

Prokeimenon, Third Tone: My soul doth magnify the Lord, and my spirit hath rejoiced in God my Saviour.

Stichos: For He hath looked upon the lowliness of His handmaiden; for behold, from henceforth all generations shall call me blessed.

Alleluia, Eighth Tone: Arise, O Lord, into Thy rest, Thou and the ark of Thy holiness.

Stichos: The Lord hath sworn in truth unto David, and He will not annul it.

Communion Verse: Receive ye the Body of Christ....

ON WEDNESDAY OF BRIGHT WEEK.

Prokeimenon, Sixth Tone: I shall commemorate thy name in every generation and generation.

Stichos: Hearken O daughter, and see, and incline thine ear.

Alleluia, Third Tone: My soul doth magnify the Lord, and my spirit hath rejoiced in God my Saviour.

Stichos: For He hath looked upon the lowliness of His handmaiden; for behold, from henceforth all generations shall call me blessed.

Communion Verse: Receive ye the Body of Christ....

ON THURSDAY OF BRIGHT WEEK:

Prokeimenon, Third Tone: O chant unto our God, chant ye; chant unto our King, chant ye.

Stichos: Clap your hands all ye nations; shout unto God with a voice of rejoicing.

Alleluia, Fourth Tone: Bend Thy bow, and proceed prosperously, and be king, because of truth and meekness and righteousness.

Stichos: Thou hast loved righteousness and hated iniquity.

Communion Verse: Receive ye the Body of Christ....

ON FRIDAY OF BRIGHT WEEK:
The Feast of the Life-giving Fount
Troparion, Third Tone:

As a life-giving fount thou didst conceive

the Dew that is transcendent in essence, O Virgin Maid. And thou didst pour forth for us the Immortal Nectar. And as ever-flowing streams from thy fountain, thou broughtest forth the Water that springeth up unto life everlasting; wherein, taking delight, we all cry out: Rejoice, O life-bearing fount.

Kontakion, Eighth Tone: From thine unfailing fount, O Maiden full of grace, thou dost reward me by pouring forth of the unending streams of thy grace that doth pass human understanding. And since thou didst bear the Word incomprehensible, I entreat thee to refresh me with thy grace divine, that I may cry to thee: Rejoice, O water of salvation.

Prokeimenon, Eighth Tone: Their sound hath gone forth into all the earth, and their words unto the ends of the world.

Stichos: The heavens declare the glory of God, and the firmament proclaimeth the work of His hands.

And the Prokeimenon, Third Tone, the Song of the Theotokos: My soul doth magnify the Lord, and my spirit hath rejoiced in God my Saviour.

Alleluia, First Tone: The heavens shall confess Thy wonders, O Lord.

Stichos: God Who is glorified in the council of the saints.

Stichos: Hearken, O daughter, and see, and incline thine ear.

Communion Verse: Receive ye the Body of Christ....

And: I will take the cup of salvation, and I will call upon the name of the Lord.

ON SATURDAY OF BRIGHT WEEK:

Prokeimenon, Third Tone: The Lord is my light and my saviour; whom then shall I fear?

Stichos: The Lord is the defender of my life; of whom then shall I be afraid?

Alleluia, Fifth Tone: The Lord is King, He is clothed with majesty; the Lord is clothed with strength and He hath girt Himself.

Stichos: For He established the world which shall not be shaken.

Communion Verse: Receive ye the Body of Christ....

THE SECOND SUNDAY OF PASCHA:
Thomas Sunday.

Troparion, Seventh Tone:
While the tomb was sealed, Thou, O Life, didst shine forth from the grave, O Christ God. And while the doors were shut, Thou didst come unto Thy disciples, O Resurrection of all, renewing through them an upright Spirit in us according to Thy great mercy.

Kontakion, Eighth Tone: With his searching right hand, Thomas did probe Thy life-bearing side, O Christ God; for when Thou didst enter while the doors were shut, he cried out unto Thee with the rest of the disciples: Thou art my Lord and my God.

Prokeimenon, Third Tone: Great is our Lord, and great is His strength, and of His understanding there is no measure.

Stichos: Praise ye the Lord, for a psalm is a good thing; let praise be sweet unto our God.

Alleluia, Eighth Tone: Come let us rejoice in the Lord, let us shout with jubilation unto God our Saviour.

Stichos: For the Lord is a great God and a great king over all the earth.

Communion Verse: Praise the Lord, O Jerusalem; praise thy God, O Sion. *(Ps. 147:1)*

THE THIRD SUNDAY OF PASCHA:
The Sunday of the Myrrh-bearers

Troparia, Second Tone: When Thou didst descend unto death, O Life Immortal, then didst Thou slay hades with the lightning of Thy Divinity.   And when Thou didst also raise the dead out of the nethermost depths, all the hosts of the heavens cried out: O Life-giver, Christ our God, glory be to Thee.

The noble Joseph, taking Thine immaculate Body down from the Tree, and having wrapped It in pure linen and spices, laid It in a new tomb. But on the third day Thou didst arise, O Lord, granting to the world great mercy.

Unto the myrrh-bearing women did the angel cry out as he stood by the tomb: Myrrh is meet for the dead, but Christ hath proved to be a stranger to corruption. But cry out: The Lord is risen, granting to the world great mercy.

Kontakion, Second Tone: When Thou didst cry, Rejoice, unto the myrrh-bearers, Thou didst make the lamentation of Eve the first mother to cease by Thy Resurrection, O Christ God.

And Thou didst bid Thine apostles to preach: The Saviour is risen from the grave.

Prokeimenon, Sixth Tone: Save, O Lord, Thy people and bless Thine inheritance.

Stichos: Unto Thee, O Lord, will I cry; O my God, be not silent unto me.

Alleluia, Eighth Tone: Thou hast been gracious, O Lord, unto Thy land; Thou hast turned back the captivity of Jacob.

Stichos: Mercy and truth are met together, righteousness and peace have kissed each other.

Communion Verse: Receive ye the Body of Christ.... **Another:** Praise the Lord from the heavens, praise Him in the highest.

THE FOURTH SUNDAY OF PASCHA:
The Sunday of the Paralytic

Troparion, Third Tone: Let the heavens be glad; let earthly things rejoice; for the Lord hath wrought might with His arm. He hath trampled down death by death; the first-born of the dead hath He become. From the belly of hades hath He delivered us and hath granted the world great mercy.

Kontakion, Third Tone: As of old Thou didst raise the paralytic, O Lord, by Thy Divine presence, raise my soul which is paralyzed grievously by all manner of sins and unseemly deeds, that being saved I may cry out: O compasionate Christ, glory be to Thy power.

Prokeimenon, First Tone: Let Thy mercy, O Lord, be upon us according as we have hoped in Thee.

Stichos: Rejoice in the Lord, O ye righteous, praise is meet for the upright.

Alleluia, Fifth Tone: Of Thy mercies, O Lord, will I sing for ever, unto generation and generation. *(Ps.88:1)*

Stichos: For Thou. hast said: Mercy shall be built up for ever. *(Ps.88:2)*

Communion Verse: Receive ye the Body of Christ.... **Another:** Praise the Lord from the heavens, praise Him in the highest.

ON WEDNESDAY OF MID-PENTECOST:

Troparion, Eighth Tone: In the midst of the Feast, give Thou my thirsty soul to drink of the waters of piety; for Thou, O Saviour, didst cry out to all: Whosoever is thirsty, let him come to Me and drink. Wherefore, O Well-spring of life, Christ our God, glory be to Thee.

Kontakion, Fourth Tone: In the midst of

the Judaic feast, Thou didst say to those present, O Christ God, Master and Creator of all: Come ye, and receive the Water of immortality. Wherefore, we fall down before Thee, crying out in faith and saying: Grant us Thy mercy and compassion; for Thou art the wellspring of our life.

Prokeimenon, Third Tone: Great is our Lord, and great is His strength, and of His understanding there is no measure.

Stichos: But God is our king before the ages, He hath wrought salvation in the midst of the earth.

Communion Verse: He that eateth My Flesh, and drinketh My Blood abideth in Me, and I in him, saith the Lord.

THE FIFTH SUNDAY OF PASCHA:
The Sunday of the Samaritan Woman

Troparion, Fourth Tone: Having learned the joyful proclamation of the Resurrection from the angel, and having cast off the ancestral condemnation, the women disciples of the Lord spake to the apostles exultantly: Death is despoiled and Christ God is risen, granting to the world great mercy.

Kontakion, Eighth Tone: Having come to the well in faith, the Samaritan woman saw Thee, the Water of Wisdom, whereof having drunk abundantly, she, the renowned one, inherited the kingdom on high for ever.

Prokeimenon, Third Tone: O chant unto our God, chant ye; chant unto our King, chant ye.

Stichos: Clap your hands, all ye nations; shout unto God with a voice of rejoicing.

Alleluia, Fourth Tone: Bend Thy bow, and proceed prosperously and be king, because of truth and meekness and righteousness.

Stichos: Thou hast loved righteousness and hated iniquity

Communion Verse: Receive ye the Body of Christ.... **Another:** Praise the Lord from the heavens, praise Him in the highest.

THE SIXTH SUNDAY OF PASCHA:
The Sunday of the Blind Man.

Troparion, Fifth Tone: Let us, O faithful, praise and worship the Word Who is co-unoriginate with the Father and the Spirit, and Who was born of the Virgin for our salvation; for He was pleased to ascend the Cross in the flesh and to endure death, and to raise the dead by His glorious Resurrection.

Kontakion, Fourth Tone: Blinded in the eyes of my soul, I draw nigh unto Thee, O Christ, like the man blind from his birth, and in repentance I cry to Thee: Thou art the exceeding radiant Light of those in darkness.

Prokeimenon, Eighth Tone: Make your vows and pay them to the Lord our God.

Stichos: In Judea is God known, His name is great in Israel.

Alleluia, Eighth Tone: Look upon me and have mercy on me

Stichos: My steps do Thou direct according to Thy saying.

Communion Verse: Receive ye the Body of Christ... **Another:** Praise the Lord from the heavens....

ON THURSDAY OF THE SIXTH WEEK
THE ASCENSION OF THE LORD
THE FIRST ANTIPHON, Psalm 46, Second Tone:

Stichos 1: Clap your hands, all ye nations; shout unto God with a voice of rejoicing.

Refrain: Through the prayers of the Theotokos, O Saviour, save us.

Stichos 2: For the Lord Most High is terrible, a great King over all the earth. *Refrain.*

Stichos 3: He hath subdued peoples under us, and nations under our feet. *Refrain.*

Stichos 4: God is gone up in jubilation, the Lord with the voice of the trumpet. *Refrain.*

Glory to the Father, and to the Son, and to the Holy Spirit, both now and ever, and unto the ages of ages. Amen. *Refrain.*

THE SECOND ANTIPHON, Psalm 47, Second Tone:

Stichos 1: Great is the Lord, and greatly to be praised, in the city of our God, in His holy mountain.

Refrain: O Son of God, Who didst ascend in glory, save us who chant unto Thee: Alleluia.

Stichos 2: The mountains of Sion on the sides of the north, the city of the great King. *Refrain.*

Stichos 3: God is known in her towers, when He cometh to help her. *Refrain.*

Stichos 4: For lo, the kings of the earth were assembled; they came together. *Refrain.*

Glory,... both now.... O Only-begotten Son and Word of God, Who art immortal....

THE THIRD ANTIPHON, Psalm 48, Fourth Tone:

Stichos 1 *(Reader)*: Hear this, all ye nations; give ear, all ye that inhabit the world.

CHOIR, the **Troparion, Fourth Tone:**

Thou hast ascended in glory, O Christ our God, having gladdened Thy disciples with the promise of the Holy Spirit; and they were assured by the blessing that Thou art the Son of God, the Redeemer of the world.

Stichos 2: Both ye that are born of earth, and ye sons of men, rich and poor together. *Troparion.*

Stichos 3: My mouth shall speak wisdom, and the meditation of my heart shall be of under standing. *Troparion.*

Stichos 4: I will incline mine ear unto a parable, I will unfold my problem on the psaltery. *Troparion.*

At the Small Entry. the Verse (said by deacon /priest): God is gone up in jubilation, the Lord with the voice of the trumpet.

CHOIR, the **Troparion, Fourth Tone:**

Thou hast ascended in glory, O Christ our God, having gladdened Thy disciples with the promise of the Holy Spirit; and they were assured by the blessing that Thou art the Son of God, the Redeemer of the world.

Kontakion, Sixth Tone:

When Thou didst fulfill Thy dispensation for our sake, uniting things on earth with the heavens, Thou didst ascend in glory, O Christ our God, departing not hence, but remaining inseparable from us, and crying unto them that love Thee: I am with you, and no one shall be against you.

Prokeimenon, Seventh Tone: Be Thou exalted above the heavens, O God, and Thy glory above all the earth.

Stichos: Ready is my heart, O God, ready is my heart; I will sing and chant in my glory.

Alleluia, Second Tone: God is gone up in jubilation, the Lord with the voice of the trumpet.

Stichos: Clap your hands, all ye nations; shout unto God with a voice of rejoicing.

Instead of It is truly meet, *we chant the Eirmos of the 9th Ode of the first canon of the feast, Fifth Tone:*

Refrain: Magnify, O my soul, Him Who hath ascended from earth to heaven, Christ the Giver of life.

Eirmos: Thee that art above understanding and word the Mother of God, that hast ineffably brought forth in time the Timeless One, we the faithful with one accord magnify.

Communion Verse: God is gone up in jubilation, the Lord with the voice of the trumpet.

THE SEVENTH SUNDAY OF PASCHA:
Sunday of the Holy Fathers

Troparion, Sixth Tone: Angelic hosts were above Thy tomb, and they that guarded Thee became as dead. And Mary stood by the grave seeking Thine immaculate Body. Thou didst despoil hades and wast not tempted by it. Thou didst meet the Virgin and didst grant us life. O Thou Who didst rise from the dead, O Lord, glory be to Thee.

Troparion to the Holy Fathers, Eighth Tone:

Most glorified art Thou, O Christ our God, Who hast established our holy fathers as luminous stars upon the earth, and through them didst guide us all to the true Faith. O Most merciful One, glory be to Thee.

Kontakion to the Holy Fathers, Eighth Tone:

The preaching of the apostles and the doctrines of the fathers confirmed the one Faith of the Church. And wearing the garment of truth, woven from the theology on high, She rightly divideth and glorifieth the great mystery of piety.

Prokeimenon, Fourth Tone, the Song of the Fathers: Blessed art Thou, O Lord, the God of our fathers, and praised and glorified is Thy name unto the ages.

Stichos: For righteous art Thou in all which Thou hast done for us.

Alleluia, First Tone: The God of gods, the Lord, hath spoken, and He hath called the earth from the rising of the sun and unto the setting thereof.

Stichos: Gather together unto Him His holy ones who have established His covenant upon sacrifices.

Communion Verse: Praise the Lord from the heavens.... **Another:** Rejoice in the Lord, O ye righteous; praise is meet for the upright.

ON SATURDAY BEFORE PENTECOST:
Commemoration of the Departed

Troparion, Eighth Tone: O Thou Who by the depth of Thy wisdom dost provide all things out of love for man, and grantest unto all that which is profitable, O only Creator; Grant rest, O Lord, to the souls of Thy servants; for in Thee have they placed their hope, O our Creator and Fashioner and God.

Glory: Kontakion, Eighth Tone: With the saints give rest, O Christ, to the souls of Thy servants, where there is neither sickness, nor sorrow, nor sighing, but life everlasting.

Both now: Theotokion: In thee we have a wall and a haven, and an intercessor acceptable to God Whom thou didst bear, O Theotokos unwedded, salvation of the faithful.

Prokeimenon, Sixth Tone: Their souls shall dwell among good things.

Stichos: Unto Thee, O Lord, have I lifted up my soul. O my God, in Thee have I trusted; let me never be put to shame.

Alleluia, Sixth Tone: Blessed are they whom Thou hast chosen and hast taken to Thyself; O Lord, and their memorial is unto generation and generation.

Stichos: Their souls shall dwell among good

things.

Communion Verse: Blessed are they whom Thou hast chosen and hast taken to Thyself, O Lord, and their memorial is unto generation and generation.

THE SUNDAY OF HOLY PENTECOST
THE FIRST ANTIPHON, Psalm 18, Second Tone:

Stichos 1: The heavens declare the glory of God, and the firmament declareth the work of His hands.

Refrain: Through the prayers of the Theotokos, O Saviour, save us.

Stichos 2: Day unto day poureth forth speech and night unto night proclaimeth knowledge. *Refrain.*

Stichos 3: Their sound hath gone forth into all the earth, and their words unto the ends of the world. *Refrain.*

Glory to the Father, and to the Son, and to the Holy Spirit, both now and ever, and unto the ages of ages. Amen. *Refrain.*

THE SECOND ANTIPHON, Psalm 19, Second Tone:

Stichos 1: The Lord hear thee in the day

of affliction; the name of the God of Jacob defend thee.

Refrain: O Good Comforter, save us who chant unto Thee: Alleluia.

Stichos 2: Let Him send forth unto thee help from His sanctuary, and out of Sion let Him help thee. *Refrain.*

Stichos 3: The Lord grant thee according to thy heart, and fulfill all thy purposes. *Refrain.*

Glory to the Father, and to the Son, and to the Holy Spirit, both now and ever, and unto the ages of ages. Amen.

O Only-begotten Son and Word of God,...

THE THIRD ANTIPHON, Psalm 20, Eighth Tone:

Stichos 1 *(Reader):* O Lord, in Thy strength the king shall be glad, and in Thy salvation shall he rejoice exceedingly.

CHOIR, the **Troparion, Eighth Tone:**

Blessed art Thou, O Christ our God, Who hast shown forth the fishermen as supremely wise, by sending down upon them the Holy Spirit, and through them didst draw the world into Thy net. O Lover of mankind, glory be to Thee.

Stichos 2: The desire of his heart hast Thou granted unto him, and hast not denied him the requests of his lips. *Troparion.*

Stichos 3: Thou wentest before him with the blessings of goodness, Thou hast set upon his head a crown of precious stone. *Troparion.*

At the Small Entry, the Verse (said by deacon/ priest): Be Thou exalted, O Lord, in Thy strength; we will sing and chant of Thy mighty acts. *(Ps. 20:13)*

CHOIR, the **Troparion, Eighth Tone:**

Blessed art Thou, O Christ our God,* Who hast shown forth the fishermen as supremely wise,* by sending down upon them the Holy Spirit,* and through them didst draw the world into Thy net.* O Lover of mankind, glory be to Thee.

Glory to the Father, and to the Son, and to the Holy Spirit, both now and ever, and unto the ages of ages. Amen.

Kontakion, Eighth Tone:

Once, when He descended and confounded the tongues,* the Most High divided the nations;* and when He divided the tongues of fire,* He called all men into unity;* and with one accord we glorify the All-Holy Spirit.

Instead of the Trisagion: As many as have been baptized into Christ have put on Christ. Alleluia. *Thrice.*

Glory to the Father, and to the Son, and to the Holy Spirit, both now and ever, and unto the ages of ages. Amen. Have put on Christ. Alleluia.

As many as have been baptized into Christ have put on Christ. Alleluia.

Prokeimenon, Eighth Tone: Their sound hath gone forth into all the earth, and their words unto the ends of the world.

Stichos: The heavens declare the glory, of God, and the firmament proclaimeth the work of His hands.

Alleluia, First Tone: By the Word of the Lord were the heavens established, and all the might of them by the Spirit of His mouth.

Stichos: The Lord looked down from heaven, He beheld all the sons of men.

Instead of It is truly meet *we chant the Eirmos of the 9th Ode of the second canon, Fourth Tone:*

Rejoice, thou, O Queen, the glory of both mothers and virgins! For no mouth, however fluent and well-spoken, can be so eloquent as to hymn thee worthily; and every mind faileth to understand thy childbirth. Wherefore, with one accord thee do we glorify.

Communion Verse: Thy good Spirit shall lead me in the land of uprightness. *(Ps. 142:12)*

THE FIRST SUNDAY AFTER PENTECOST:
The Sunday of All Saints

Troparion, Eighth Tone: From on high didst Thou descend, O Compassionate One; to burial of three days hast Thou submitted that Thou mightest free us from our passions. O our Life and Resurrection, O Lord, glory be to Thee.

Troparion to All Saints, Fourth Tone:

Adorned in the blood of Thy martyrs throughout all the world, as in purple and fine linen, Thy Church, through them, doth cry unto Thee, O Christ God: Send down Thy compassions upon Thy people; grant peace to Thy flock and to our souls great mercy.

Glory. Both now. Kontakion to All Saints, Eighth Tone: To Thee, O Lord, the Planter of creation, the world doth offer the God-bearing martyrs as the first-fruits of nature. By their intercessions, preserve Thy Church, Thy commonwealth, in profound peace, through the Theotokos, O Greatly-merciful One.

Prokeimenon, Eighth Tone: Make your vows and pay them to the Lord our God.

Stichos: In Judea is God known, His name is great in Israel.

And the Prokeimenon for All Saints, Fourth Tone: Wondrous is God in His saints, the God of Israel.

Alleluia, Fourth Tone: The righteous cried, and the Lord heard them.

Stichos: Many are the tribulations of the righteous, and the Lord shall deliver them out of them all.

Communion Verse: Praise the Lord from the heavens, praise Him in the highest.

Another: Rejoice in the Lord, O ye righteous; praise is meet for the upright.

SECOND SUNDAY AFTER PENTECOST:
The Sunday of All Saints of Russia, and All Saints of Mount Athos
Troparion of the Resurrection, First Tone:
When the stone had been sealed by the Jews, and the soldiers were guarding Thine

immaculate Body, Thou didst rise on the third day, O Saviour, granting life unto the world. Wherefore, the Hosts of the heavens cried out to Thee, O Life-giver: Glory to Thy Resurrection, O Christ. Glory to Thy kingdom. Glory to Thy dispensation, O only Lover of mankind.

Troparion to All Saints of Russia, Eighth Tone: As a beautiful fruit of the sowing of Thy salvation, the land of Russia doth offer to Thee, O Lord, all the Saints that have shone in her. By their prayers keep the Church and the world in profound peace, through the Theotokos, O Most-merciful One.

Troparion to All Saints of Mount Athos, First Tone: With hymns and songs let us honour the fathers of Athos, those angels in the flesh, the confessors, the righteous ones, the hierarchs, and the martyrs. And let us, the whole multitude of monastics, emulate their virtues and cry out with one voice: Glory to Him that hath crowned you. Glory to Him that hath sanctified you. Glory to Him that hath shown you forth as our protectors in perils.

Kontakion of the Resurrection, First Tone: As God Thou didst arise from the tomb in glory, and Thou didst raise the world together with Thyself. And mortal nature praiseth Thee as God, and death hath vanished. And Adam danceth, O Master, and Eve, now freed from fetters, rejoiceth as she crieth out: Thou art He, O Christ, that grantest unto all resurrection.

Kontakion to All Saints of Russia, Third Tone:

Today the choir of the saints who pleased God in the land of Russia doth stand before us in church and invisibly doth pray for us to God. With them the angels glorify Him, and all the saints of the Church of Christ keep festival with them; and they all pray together for us to the Eternal God.

Kontakion to All Saints of Mount Athos, Fourth Tone: Let us all praise the fathers who have made the Holy Mount like unto heaven, and who have shone forth in this life like angels and who did gather a great multitude of monastics there; and let us cry unto them: Deliver us from every necessity and the attacks of the evil one, O thou multitude of monastic saints, thou boast and joy of Athos.

Prokeimenon, First Tone: Let Thy mercy, O Lord, be upon us, according as we have hoped in Thee.

Stichos: Rejoice in the Lord, O ye righteous; praise is meet for the upright.

And the Prokeimenon for All Saints of Russia, Seventh Tone: Precious in the sight of the Lord is the death of His saints.

Alleluia, First Tone: O God Who givest avengement unto me and hast subdued peoples under me.

Stichos: It is He that magnifieth the salvation of His king and worketh mercy for His anointed, for David and for his seed unto eternity.

Stichos: Be glad in the Lord, and rejoice, ye righteous.

Communion Verse: Praise the Lord from the heavens, praise Him in the highest.

Another: Rejoice in the Lord, O ye righteous; praise is meet for the upright.

THE END OF THE PENTECOSTARION

❄❄❄❄❄❄

THE MENAION SERVICES
(FEASTS OF THE IMMOVABLE CALENDAR)
8 SEPTEMBER: THE NATIVITY OF OUR MOST HOLY LADY THE THEOTOKOS AND EVER-VIRGIN MARY.

Troparion, Fourth Tone:

Thy nativity, O Theotokos Virgin,* hath proclaimed joy to all the world;* for from thee hath dawned the Sun of Righteousness, Christ our God,* annulling the curse, and bestowing the blessing,* abolishing death and granting us life eternal.

Kontakion, Fourth Tone:

Joachim and Anna were freed from the reproach of childlessness* and Adam and Eve from the corruption of death, by thy holy nativity, O immaculate one,* which thy people, redeemed from the guilt of offences,* celebrate, by crying to thee:* The barren woman giveth birth to the Theotokos, the nourisher of our life.

Prokeimenon, Third Tone, the Song of the Theotokos: My soul doth magnify the Lord, and my spirit hath rejoiced in God my Saviour.

Stichos: For He hath looked upon the lowliness of His handmaiden; for behold, from henceforth all generations shall call me blessed.

Alleluia, Eighth Tone: Hearken, O daughter, and see, and incline thine ear.

Stichos: The rich among the people shall entreat thy countenance.

Instead of It is truly meet, *we chant the Eirmos of the 9th Ode of the second canon, Eighth Tone:*

Refrain: Magnify, O my soul, the most glorious nativity of the Mother of God.

Eirmos: Foreign to mothers is virginity, and strange is childbirth for virgins, yet both were accomplished in thee, O Theotokos. Wherefore, we and all generations of the earth without ceasing do magnify thee.

Communion Verse: I will take the cup of salvation, and I will call upon the name of the Lord.

14 SEPTEMBER: THE UNIVERSAL EXALTATION OF THE PRECIOUS AND LIFE-GIVING CROSS.

THE FIRST ANTIPHON, Psalm 21, Second Tone:

Stichos 1: O God, my God, attend to me;

why hast Thou forsaken me?

Refrain: Through the prayers of the Theotokos, O Saviour, save us.

Stichos 2: Far from my salvation are the words of my transgressions. *Refrain.*

Stichos 3: My God, I will cry by day, and wilt Thou not hearken? and by night, and it shall not be unto folly for me. *Refrain.*

Stichos 4: But as for Thee, Thou dwellest, in the sanctuary, O Praise of Israel. *Refrain.*

Glory to the Father, and to the Son, and to the Holy Spirit, both now, and ever, and unto the ages, of ages, Amen. *Refrain.*

THE SECOND ANTIPHON, Psalm 73, Second Tone:

Stichos: 1: O God, why hast Thou cast us off unto the end?

Refrain: O Son of God, Who wast crucified in the flesh, save us who chant unto Thee: Alleluia.

Stichos 2: Remember Thy congregation which Thou hast purchased from the beginning. *Refrain.*

Stichos 3: This is Mount Sion wherein Thou hast dwelt. *Refrain.*

Stichos 4: But God is our king before the ages, He hath wrought salvation in the midst of the earth. *Refrain.*

Glory to the Father, and to the Son, and to the Holy Spirit, both now and ever, and unto the ages of ages.

O Only-begotten Son and Word of God, Who art immortal....

THE THIRD ANTIPHON, Psalm 98, First Tone:

Stichos 1 *(Reader):* The Lord is king, let the peoples rage; He sitteth on the cherubim, let the earth be shaken.

CHOIR, **Troparion, First Tone:** Save, O Lord, Thy people, and bless Thine inheritance; grant Thou unto Orthodox Christians victory over enemies; and by the power of Thy Cross do Thou preserve Thy commonwealth.

Stichos 2: The Lord is great in Sion, and He is high above all peoples. *Troparion.*

Stichos 3: Worship the Lord in His holy court. *Troparion.*

At the Small Entry, the Verse (said by deacon/ priest): Exalt ye the Lord our God, and worship the footstool of His feet, for It is holy.

CHOIR, **Troparion, First Tone:**

Save, O Lord, Thy people,* and bless Thine inheritance;* grant Thou unto Orthodox Christians victory over enemies;* and by the power of Thy Cross do Thou preserve Thy commonwealth.

Kontakion, Fourth Tone:

O Thou Who wast lifted up willingly on the Cross,* bestow Thy mercies upon the new community named after Thee, O Christ God;* gladden with Thy power the Orthodox Christians,* granting them victory over enemies;* may they have as Thy help the weapon of peace, the invincible trophy.

Instead of the Trisagion: Before Thy Cross we bow down, O Master and Thy holy Resurrection we glorify. *Thrice.*

Glory to the Father, and to the Son, and to the Holy Spirit, both now and ever, and unto the ages of ages. Amen. And Thy holy Resurrection we glorify.

Before Thy Cross we bow down, O Master, and Thy holy Resurrection we glorify.

Prokeimenon, Seventh Tone: Exalt ye the Lord our God, and worship the footstool of

His feet, for It is holy.

Stichos: The Lord is king, let the peoples rage.

Alleluia, First Tone: Remember Thy congregation which Thou hast purchased from the beginning.

Stichos: But God is our king before the ages, He hath wrought salvation in the midst of the earth.

Instead of It is truly meet, *we chant the Eirmos of the 9th Ode of the first canon, Eighth Tone:*

Refrain: Magnify, O my soul, the most precious Cross of the Lord.

Eirmos: O Theotokos, thou art a mystical paradise, which being untilled brought forth Christ, by Whom the life-bringing Tree of the Cross was planted in the earth. In worshipping Him now through its exaltation, thee do we magnify.

Communion Verse: The light of Thy countenance, O Lord, hath been signed upon us.

25 SEPTEMBER: THE REPOSE OF SAINT SERGIUS OF RADONEZH.

Troparion, Fourth Tone: As a champion of the virtues, and as a true soldier of Christ

God, thou didst struggle mightily against the passions in this temporal life, and thou wast a model for thy disciples in chants, vigils, and fasting. Wherefore, the Most Holy Spirit dwelt in thee, and thou wast brightly adorned by His grace. But as thou hast boldness toward the Holy Trinity, remember the flock which thou didst gather so wisely, and forget not to visit thy children as thou didst promise, O Sergius, our holy father.

Kontakion, Eighth Tone: Wounded with love for Christ, O Saint, and having followed Him with unwaning desire, thou didst hate all carnal pleasure, and like the sun thou didst shine on thy fatherland. Wherefore, Christ hath enriched thee with the gift of wonder-working. Remember us who honour thy most illustrious memory, that we may cry to thee: Rejoice, divinely-wise Sergius.

Prokeimenon, Seventh Tone: Precious in the sight of the Lord is the death of His saints.

Stichos: What shall I render unto the Lord for all that He hath rendered unto me?

Alleluia, Sixth Tone: Blessed the man that feareth the Lord; in His commandments shall he greatly delight.

Stichos: His seed shall be mighty upon the earth.

Communion Verse: In everlasting remembrance shall the righteous be; he shall not be afraid of evil tidings.

26 SEPTEMBER: THE REPOSE OF THE HOLY APOSTLE AND EVANGELIST JOHN THE THEOLOGIAN

Troparion, Second Tone: O Apostle beloved of Christ our God, hasten to deliver a defenceless people. He that allowed thee to recline on His breast, receiveth thee bowing in intercession. Implore Him, O Theologian, to dispel the persistent cloud of the heathen, and ask for us His peace and great mercy.

Kontakion, Second Tone: Who can tell thy mighty works, O virgin Saint? For thou pourest forth miracles, and art a source of healings, and thou dost intercede for our souls, as the theologian and friend of Christ.

Prokeimenon, Eighth Tone: Their sound hath gone forth into all the earth and their words unto the ends of the world.

Stichos: The heavens declare the glory of

God, and the firmament proclaimeth the work of His hands.

Alleluia, First Tone: The heavens shall confess Thy wonders, O Lord, and Thy truth in the congregation of saints.

Stichos: God Who is glorified in the council of the saints.

Communion Verse: Their sound hath gone forth into all the earth, and their words unto the ends of the world.

1 OCTOBER: THE PROTECTION OF THE MOST HOLY THEOTOKOS.

Troparion, Fourth Tone: Today we Orthodox people joyfully celebrate thy glorious coming among us, O Mother of God, and gazing upon thy most pure image, we say with compunction: Shelter us with thy most precious protection, and deliver us from all evil, and pray to thy Son, Christ our God, that He save our souls.

Kontakion, Third Tone: Today the Virgin doth stand before us in church, and with the choirs of saints invisibly prayeth for us to God. Angels worship with hierarchs, apostles rejoice with prophets, for the Theotokos prayeth for us to the Eternal God.

Prokeimenon, Third Tone, the Song of the Theotokos: My soul doth magnify the Lord, and my spirit hath rejoiced in God my Saviour.

Stichos: For He hath looked upon the lowliness of His handmaiden; for behold, from henceforth all generations shall call me blessed.

Alleluia, Eighth Tone: Hearken, O daughter, and see, and incline thine ear.

Stichos: The rich among the people shall entreat thy countenance.

Communion Verse: I will take the cup of salvation, and I will call upon the name of the Lord.

10 OCTOBER: THE OPTINA ELDERS.

Troparion, First Tone: Abiding in unceasing prayer, embracing both the good and the wicked with love, O holy elders of Optina, ye did serve both God and neighbour. Through vigils, tears, and fasting ye did receive the gift of all manner of miracles. Glory to Him Who hath given us such mediators. Glory to Him Who hath glorified you. Glory to God Who is wondrous in His saints.

Kontakion, Eighth Tone: Ye who from the vanity of the world have turned away, and through purity of life found a treasury, ye did not cease to care for sinners in the world; but as ye are guides for those astray, deliver us also from the vanities of the world, that we may cry: Rejoice, O divinely-wise elders.

Prokeimenon, Seventh Tone: Precious in the sight of the Lord is the death of His saints.

Stichos: What shall I render unto the Lord for all that He hath rendered unto me?

Alleluia, Sixth Tone: Blessed is the man that feareth the Lord; in His commandments shall he greatly delight.

Communion Verse: Rejoice in the Lord, O ye righteous; praise is meet for the upright.

11 OCTOBER: COMMEMORATION OF THE HOLY FATHERS OF THE SEVENTH ECUMENICAL COUNCIL.

If this date fall on Wednesday or earlier, the Fathers are commemorated on the preceding Sunday. If on Thursday or later, then on the following Sunday.

Troparion of the Resurrection, and then to the Holy Fathers, Eighth Tone: Most glorified art Thou, O Christ our, God, Who hast established our holy fathers as luminous stars upon the earth, and through them didst guide us all to the true Faith. O Most-merciful one, glory be to Thee.

Kontakion of the Resurrection. Glory: Kontakion to the Holy Fathers, Sixth Tone: The Son Who shined forth from the Father ineffably was born, twofold of nature, of a woman. Knowing Him, we deny not the image of His form; but depicting it piously, we revere it faithfully. And for this cause, the Church, in that it holdeth the true Faith, doth kiss the icon of Christ's incarnation.

Both now: *The Kontakion of the temple, or* O Protection of Christians....

Prokeimenon of the Tone, then the Song of the Fathers, Fourth Tone: Blessed art Thou, O Lord, the God of our fathers, and praised and glorified is Thy name unto the ages.

Alleluia of the Tone, and of the Fathers, First Tone: The God of gods, the Lord, hath spoken, and He hath called the earth from the rising of the sun and unto the setting thereof.

Communion Verse: Praise the Lord from the heavens, praise Him in the highest.

Another: Rejoice in the Lord, O ye righteous; praise is meet for the upright.

19 OCTOBER: ST. JOHN OF KRONSTADT.

Troparion, Fourth Tone: O Wonderworker living in Christ forever,* with love have mercy on them that are in danger;* hear thy children who call upon thee with faith;* be thou compassionate unto them that hope for aid from thee,* O Father John of Kronstadt, our beloved shepherd.

Kontakion, Fourth Tone: O thou who from infancy wast chosen by God, and in childhood didst miraculously receive from Him the gift of learning, and wast gloriously called to the priesthood in a vision during sleep, thou didst prove to be a wonderful shepherd of the Church of Christ, O Father John, namesake of grace. Pray to Christ our God that we all be with thee in the kingdom of the heavens.

Prokeimenon, Seventh Tone: The righteous man shall be glad in the Lord, and shall hope in Him. *(Ps.6:11)*

Alleluia, Fourth Tone: His heart is ready to hope in the Lord. *(Ps.111:7)*

Stichos: A good man is he that is compassionate and lendeth. *(Ps.111:5)*

Communion Verse: In everlasting remembrance shall the righteous be; he shall not be afraid of evil tidings.

22 OCTOBER: THE KAZAN ICON OF THE MOST HOLY THEOTOKOS.

Troparion, Fourth Tone: O fervent intercessor, Mother of the Lord Most High, thou prayest for all to thy Son, Christ our God, and thou contrivest to save all who have recourse to thy powerful protection. O Sovereign Lady and Queen, help and defend all of us who in troubles and trials, in pain and burdened with many sins, stand before thy most pure Icon in thy presence, and pray to thee with compunction of soul, contrition of heart, and with tears, and who have unflagging hope in thee. Grant to all what is good for us, deliverance from all evil, and save us all, O Virgin Theotokos, for thou art a divine protection to thy servants.

Kontakion, Eighth Tone: Let us run, O ye peoples, to that quiet and good harbour, to the speedy helper, to the ready and warm salvation, to the Virgin's protection. Let us hurry to prayer and hasten to repentance; for the most pure Theotokos poureth out for us unfailing mercy, anticipateth our needs with her help and delivereth from great disasters and evils her well-pleasing and God-fearing servants.

Prokeimenon, Alleluia, and Communion Verse same as for the Protection – see October 1, page 206.

28 OCTOBER: THE REPOSE OF ST. JOB OF POCHAEV.

Troparion, Fourth Tone: Having acquired the patience of thy long-suffering forefather, and having resembled the Baptist in abstinence, and having shared the divine zeal of both, thou wast vouchsafed to receive their names, and thou wast a fearless preacher of the true Faith. In this way thou didst bring a multitude of monastics to Christ, and thou didst strengthen all the people in Orthodoxy, O Job, our holy father. Pray that our souls be saved.

Kontakion, Fourth Tone: Thou wast a pillar of the true Faith, a zealot for the commandments of the Gospel, a convicter of pride, an intercessor and teacher of the humble; wherefore, ask for forgiveness of sins for them that bless thee; and do thou keep thy community unharmed, O Job, our father, who dost resemble the long-suffering patriarch.

Prokeimenon, Seventh Tone: Precious in the sight of the Lord is the death of His saints.

Stichos: What shall I render unto the Lord for all that He hath rendered unto me?

Alleluia, Sixth Tone: Blessed is the man that feareth the Lord; in His commandments shall he greatly, delight.

Stichos: His seed shall be mighty upon the earth.

Communion Verse: In everlasting remembrance shall the righteous be; he shall not be afraid of evil tidings.

8 NOVEMBER: THE SYNAXIS OF THE HOLY ARCHANGEL MICHAEL AND THE OTHER BODILESS HOSTS.

Troparion, Fourth Tone: Supreme Commanders of the Heavenly Hosts, we unworthy ones implore you that by your supplications ye will encircle us with the shelter of the wings of your immaterial glory, and guard us who fall down before you and fervently cry: Deliver us from dangers since ye are the Marshalls of the Hosts on high.

Kontakion, Second Tone: Supreme Commanders of God and ministers of the Divine Glory, and guides of men and leaders of the Bodiless Hosts, ask for what is to our profit and for great mercy, since ye are Supreme Commanders of the Bodiless Hosts.

Prokeimenon, Fourth Tone: Who maketh His angels spirits, and His ministers a flame of fire.

Stichos: Bless the Lord, O my soul; O Lord my God, Thou hast been magnified exceedingly.

Alleluia, Second Tone: Praise Him, all ye His angels; praise Him, all ye His hosts.

Stichos: For He spake, and they came to be; He commanded, and they were created.

Communion Verse: Who maketh His angels spirits, and His ministers a flame of fire.

9 NOVEMBER: ST. NECTARIUS OF PENTAPOLIS.

Troparion, First Tone: The offspring of Selyvria and the guardian of Aegina, the true friend of virtue who didst appear in the last years, O Nectarius, we faithful honor thee, as a godly servant of Christ, for thou gushest forth healings of every kind for those who piously cry out: Glory to Christ Who hath glorified thee. Glory to Him that hath made thee wondrous. Glory to Him that worketh healings for all through thee.

Kontakion, Eighth Tone: In joyfulness of heart, come let us praise with hymns the newly-shining star of the Orthodox and the newly-built bulwark of the Church; for by the working of the Spirit he was glorified and doth pour forth the abounding grace of cures upon them that cry: Rejoice, O Father Nectarius.

Prokeimenon, First Tone: My mouth shall speak wisdom, and the meditation of my heart shall be of understanding.

Stichos: Hear this, all ye nations; give ear, all ye that inhabit the world.

Alleluia, Second Tone: The mouth of the righteous shall meditate wisdom, and his tongue shall speak of judgment.

Stichos: The law of God is in his heart, and his steps shall not be tripped.

Communion Verse: In everlasting remembrance shall the righteous be; he shall not be afraid of evil tidings.

13 NOVEMBER: ST. JOHN CHRYSOSTOM.

Troparion, Eighth Tone: Grace shining forth from thy mouth like a beacon hath illumined the universe, and disclosed to the world treasures of uncovetousness, and shown us the heights of humility; but while instructing by thy words, O Father John Chrysostom, intercede with the Word, Christ our God, to save our souls.

Kontakion, Sixth Tone: From the heavens hast thou received divine grace and by thy lips thou dost teach all to worship the One God in Trinity, O John Chrysostom, all-blessed righteous one. Rightly do we acclaim thee, for thou art a teacher revealing things divine.

Prokeimenon, Alleluia, and Communion Verse same as for St. Nectarius, 9 November (see preceding page).

21 NOVEMBER: THE ENTRY OF OUR MOST HOLY LADY THEOTOKOS INTO THE TEMPLE.

Troparion, Fourth Tone:

Today is the prelude of God's good will* and the heralding of the salvation of mankind.* In the temple of God, the Virgin is presented openly,* and she proclaimeth Christ unto all.* To her, then, with a great voice let us cry aloud:* Rejoice, O thou fulfillment* of the Creator's dispensation.

Kontakion, Fourth Tone:

The most pure temple of the Saviour,* the most precious bridal-chamber and Virgin,* the sacred treasury of the glory of God,* is on this day brought into the house of the Lord,* bringing with her the grace that is in the Divine Spirit.* And the angels of God chant praise unto her:* she is the heavenly tabernacle.

Prokeimenon, Third Tone, the Song of the Theotokos: My soul doth magnify the Lord, and my spirit hath rejoiced in God my Saviour.

Stichos: For He hath looked upon the lowliness of His handmaiden; for behold, from henceforth all generations shall call me blessed.

Alleluia, Eighth Tone: Hearken, O daughter, and see, and incline thine ear.

Stichos: The rich among the people shall entreat thy countenance.

Instead of It is truly meet, we chant the Eirmos of the 9th Ode of the first canon, Fourth Tone:

Refrain: The angels beholding the entry of the most pure one were struck with wonder, seeing how the Virgin entered into the Holy of Holies.

Eirmos: Let no profane hand touch the living Ark of God, but let the lips of the faithful, chanting unceasingly the words of the angel to the Theotokos, cry out with joy: Truly art thou high above all, O pure Virgin.

Communion Verse: I will take the cup of salvation, and I will call upon the name of the Lord.

26 NOVEMBER: ST. INNOCENT OF IRKUTSK.

Troparion, Third Tone: O lamp of the Church, most luminous, thou hast enlightened this land with the rays of thy virtues. And by healing a multitude of them that came unto thy shrine with faith, thou hast glorified God. We beseech thee, O holy Father Innocent, defend with thy prayers this land from all misfortune and sorrow.

Kontakion, Fourth Tone: Praise with love,

O all ye faithful, the pastor who is the namesake of blamelessness, the preacher of the Faith to the Mongol peoples, the glory and adornment of the flock of Irkutsk; for he is the guardian of this land and an intercessor for our souls.

Prokeimenon, First Tone: My mouth shall speak wisdom, and the meditation of my heart shall be of understanding.

Stichos: Hear this, all ye nations; give ear, all ye that inhabit the world.

Alleluia, First Tone: The saints shall boast in glory, and they shall rejoice upon their beds.

Stichos: This glory shall be to all His saints.

Communion Verse: In everlasting remembrance shall the righteous be; he shall not be afraid of evil tidings.

27 NOVEMBER: KURSK ROOT ICON OF THE THEOTOKOS OF THE SIGN.

Troparion, Fourth Tone: Having obtained thee as an unassailable wall and as a fountain of miracles, O most pure Theotokos, thy servants subdue the attacks of enemies. Wherefore, we pray to thee: Grant peace to our native land, and to our souls great mercy.

Kontakion, Eighth Tone: We thy people celebrate thy venerable Icon of the Sign, O Mother of God, whereby thou didst grant thy city a wonderful victory against its enemies. Wherefore, we cry unto thee with faith: Rejoice, O Virgin, thou boast of Christians.

Prokeimenon, Alleluia, and Communion Verse same as for The Entry, November 21, page 216.

6 DECEMBER: ST. NICHOLAS THE WONDERWORKER.

Troparion, Fourth Tone: The truth of things hath revealed thee to thy flock as a rule of faith, an icon of meekness and a teacher of temperance; therefore thou hast achieved the heights by humility, riches by poverty. O Father and Hierarch Nicholas, intercede with Christ God that our souls be saved.

Kontakion, Third Tone: In Myra, O Saint, thou didst prove to be a minister of things sacred; for having fulfilled the Gospel of Christ, O righteous one, thou didst lay down thy life for thy people, and didst save the innocent from death. Wherefore, thou wast sanctified as a great initiate of the grace of God.

Prokeimenon, Seventh Tone: The righteous man shall be glad in the Lord, and shall hope in Him.

Stichos: Hearken, O God, unto my prayer, when I make supplication unto Thee.

Alleluia, Fourth Tone: Thy priests shall be clothed with righteousness, and Thy righteous shall rejoice.

Communion Verse: In everlasting remembrance shall the righteous be, he shall not be afraid of evil tidings.

11-17 DECEMBER: SUNDAY OF THE HOLY FOREFATHERS.

Troparion, Second Tone: By faith didst Thou justify the Forefathers, when through them Thou didst betroth Thyself aforetime to the Church that was from among the nations. The Saints boast in glory that from their seed there is a glorious fruit, even she that bore Thee seedlessly. By their prayers, O Christ God, save our souls.

Kontakion, Sixth Tone: A hand-wrought image ye would not worship, O thrice-blessed ones; but armed with the Indescribable Essence, ye were glorified in your ordeal by fire. Standing in the midst of the irresistible flame, ye called upon God: Speed Thou, O Compassionate One, and hasten, as Thou art merciful, to come unto our aid, for Thou art able if Thou will it.

Prokeimenon, Fourth Tone, the Song of the Fathers: Blessed art Thou, O Lord, the God of our fathers, and praised and glorified is Thy name unto the ages.

Stichos: For righteous art Thou in all which Thou hast done for us.

Alleluia, Fourth Tone: Moses and Aaron among His priests, and Samuel among them that call upon His name.

Stichos: They called upon the Lord, and He hearkened unto them.

Communion Verse: Praise the Lord from the heavens, praise Him in the highest.

Another: Rejoice in the Lord, O ye righteous; praise is meet for the upright.

12 DECEMBER: ST. HERMAN, WONDERWORKER OF ALASKA.

Troparion, Fourth Tone: Blessed ascetic of the northern wilds* and gracious intercessor for the whole world,* teacher of the Orthodox Faith* and good instructor of piety,* adornment of Alaska and joy of all America,* holy Father Herman,* pray to Christ God that He save our souls.

Kontakion, Eighth Tone: Monk of Valaam and beloved of the Mother of God,* new zealot of the desert-dwellers of old by thine ascetic labours;* having taken prayer as thy sword and shield,* thou didst reveal thyself as terrible to demons and pagan darkness.* Wherefore, we cry to thee, O Saint Herman:* Pray to Christ God that our souls be saved.

Prokeimenon, Alleluia, and Communion Verse same as for St. Job of Pochaev, see October 28, (page 212).

18-24 DECEMBER: THE SUNDAY BEFORE THE NATIVITY OF CHRIST, THE SUNDAY OF THE HOLY FATHERS.

Troparion, Second Tone: Great are the achievements of faith! In the fountain of flame, as in refreshing water, the Three Holy Children rejoiced. And the prophet Daniel proved a shepherd of lions as of sheep. By their prayers, O Christ God, save our souls.

If it be the 18th or 19th of December, we chant the Kontakion of the Holy Forefathers, page 220.

If it be the 20th through the 23rd. we chant the **Kontakion of the Forefeast of Nativity, First Tone:**

Rejoice, O Bethlehem!* Ephratha, make ready!* for behold, the Ewe hasteneth to give birth unto the Great Shepherd Whom she carrieth in her womb.* And seeing Him, the God-bearing Fathers rejoice,* and with the shepherds praise the Virgin who giveth suck.

Prokeimenon, Fourth Tone, the Song of the Fathers: Blessed art Thou, O Lord, the God of our fathers, and praised and glorified is Thy name unto the ages.

Stichos: For righteous art Thou in all which Thou hast done for us.

Alleluia, Fourth Tone: O God, with our ears have we heard, for our fathers have told us. *(Ps. 43:1)*

Stichos: Thou hast saved us from them that afflict us, and them that hate us hast Thou put to shame. *(Ps. 43:8)*

Communion Verse: Praise the Lord from the heavens.... **Another:** Rejoice in the Lord, O ye righteous; praise is meet for the upright.

20 DECEMBER: THE FOREFEAST OF

THE HOLY NATIVITY and ST. JOHN OF KRONSTADT. *(See 19 October, page 209 for St. John's troparion, etc.)*

Troparion of the Forefeast, Fourth Tone:
Make ready, O Bethlehem,* Eden hath been opened unto all.* Prepare, O Ephratha,* for the Tree of life hath blossomed in the cave from the Virgin.* For her womb proved to be a spiritual paradise wherefrom there came the Divine Plant,* whereof eating we shall live and not die like Adam.* Christ is born to raise the image that fell of old.

Kontakion of the Forefeast, Third Tone:
Today the Virgin cometh to the cave to give birth ineffably to the Word Who was before the ages. Dance, O earth, at the message! Give glory with the angels and shepherds unto Him Who was willing to be gazed upon as a young child and is pre-eternal God.

24 DECEMBER: THE EVE OF THE NATIVITY OF CHRIST

Troparion, Fourth Tone: Once Mary, being with child by a seedless conception,* was registered in Bethlehem with the aged Joseph* as being of the seed of David.* The time came for the birth, and there was no room in the inn;* but the cave proved a delightful palace for the Queen.* Christ is born to raise the image that fell of old.

Kontakion: *(see the Kontakion of the Forefeast, preceding page).*

Prokeimenon First Tone: The Lord said unto Me: Thou art My Son, this day have I begotten Thee. *(Ps. 2:7)*

Stichos: Ask of Me, and I will give Thee the nations for Thine inheritance, and the uttermost parts of the earth for Thy possession.

Alleluia. Fifth Tone: The Lord said unto my Lord: Sit Thou at My right hand until I make Thine enemies the footstool of Thy feet.

Stichos: A sceptre of power shall the Lord send unto Thee out of Sion. *(Ps. 109:2)*

Stichos: From the womb before the morning star have I begotten Thee.

Communion Verse: Praise the Lord from the heavens, praise Him in the highest.

25 DECEMBER: THE NATIVITY ACCORDING TO THE FLESH OF OUR LORD GOD AND SAVIOUR JESUS CHRIST.

THE FIRST ANTIPHON, Psalm 110, Second Tone:

Stichos 1: I will confess Thee, O Lord, with my whole heart, I will tell of all Thy wonders.

Refrain: Through the prayers of the Theotokos, O Saviour, save us.

Stichos 2: In the Council of the upright and in the congregation, great are the works of the Lord. *Refrain.*

Stichos 3: Sought out in all the things that He hath willed. *Refrain.*

Stichos 4: Confession and majesty are His work, and His righteousness abideth unto ages of ages. *Refrain.*

Glory to the Father, and to the Son, and to the Holy Spirit, both now and ever, and unto the ages of ages. Amen. *Refrain.*

THE SECOND ANTIPHON, Psalm 111, Second Tone:

Stichos 1: Blessed is the man that feareth the Lord; in His commandments shall he greatly delight.

Refrain: O Son of God Who wast born of the Virgin, save us who chant unto Thee: Alleluia.

Stichos 2: His seed shall be mighty upon the earth; the generation of the upright shall be blessed. *Refrain.*

Stichos 3: Glory and riches shall be in his house, and his righteousness abideth unto ages of ages. *Refrain.*

Stichos 4: There hath risen up in darkness a light for the upright; he is merciful and compassionate and righteous. *Refrain.*

Glory to the Father, and to the Son, and to the Holy Spirit, both now and ever, and unto the ages of ages. Amen.

O Only-begotten Son and Word of God, Who art immortal....

THE THIRD ANTIPHON, Psalm 109, Fourth Tone.

Stichos 1 *(Reader):* The Lord said unto my Lord: Sit Thou at My right hand.

CHOIR, **Troparion, Fourth Tone:**

Thy Nativity, O Christ our God,* hath shined upon the world the light of knowledge;* for thereby, they that worshipped the stars* were taught by a star* to worship Thee, the Sun of Righteousness,* and to know Thee, the Dayspring from on high.* O Lord, glory be to Thee.

Stichos 2: Until I make Thine enemies the footstool of Thy feet. *Troparion.*

Stichos 3: A sceptre of power shall the Lord send unto Thee out of Sion; rule Thou in the midst of Thine enemies. *Troparion.*

Stichos 4: With Thee is dominion in the day of Thy power, in the splendour of Thy saints. *Troparion.*

At the Small Entry, the Verse (said by the deacon/priest): From the womb before the morning star have I begotten Thee. The Lord hath sworn and will not repent: Thou art a priest forever, after the order of Melchisedek.

CHOIR: Thy Nativity, O Christ our God.... *(see preceding page).* Glory. Both now.

Kontakion, Third Tone:

Today the Virgin giveth birth to Him Who is transcendent in essence;* and the earth offereth a cave to Him Who is unapproachable.* Angels with shepherds give glory;* with a star the Magi do journey;* for our sake a young Child is born, Who is pre-eternal God.

Instead of the Trisagion: As many as have been baptized into Christ have put on Christ. Alleluia. *Thrice.*

Glory to the Father, and to the Son, and to the Holy Spirit, both now and ever, and unto the ages of ages. Amen. Have put on Christ. Alleluia.

As many as have been baptized into Christ have put on Christ. Alleluia.

Prokeimenon, Eighth Tone: Let all the earth worship Thee and chant unto Thee; let them chant unto Thy name, O Most High.

Stichos: Shout with jubilation unto the Lord all the earth; chant ye unto His name, give glory in praise of Him. *(Ps.65:1)*

Alleluia, First Tone: The heavens declare the glory of God, and the firmament proclaimeth the work of His hands.

Stichos: Day unto day poureth forth speech, and night unto night proclaimeth knowledge.

Instead of It is truly meet, we chant the Eirmos of the 9th Ode of the second canon of the feast, First Tone:

Refrain: Magnify, O my soul, her who is more honourable and more glorious than the hosts on high, the most pure Virgin Theotokos.

Eirmos: It would be easier for us, because

free from all danger, to keep silence in fear; while it is hard indeed, O Virgin, to devise with love hymns harmoniously put together. But do thou, O Mother, grant us power that we may fulfill our good intent.

According to some current usage, the Eirmos of the first canon, same tone, is used instead:

A mystery strange and most glorious do I see: The cave is heaven; the Virgin the throne of the cherubim; the manger the room in which was laid the uncontainable Christ God, Whom we do hymn and magnify.

Communion Verse: The Lord hath sent redemption unto His people. *(Ps.110:8)*

26 DECEMBER: THE SECOND DAY OF NATIVITY: THE SYNAXIS OF THE MOST HOLY THEOTOKOS.

At the Small Entry: O come let us worship and fall down before Christ; O Son of God Who wast born of the Virgin, save us who chant unto Thee: Alleluia.

Troparion of the Feast. Glory. Both now.

Kontakion Sixth Tone: He that was born before the morning star of Father without mother, is today on earth incarnate of thee without father. A star calleth the glad tidings to the Magi; while angels and shepherds praise thy seedless childbirth, O thou who art full of grace.

Prokeimenon, Third Tone, the Song of the Theotokos: My soul doth magnify the Lord, and my spirit hath rejoiced in God my Saviour.

Stichos: For He hath looked upon the lowliness of His handmaiden; for behold, from henceforth all generations shall call me blessed.

Alleluia, Eighth Tone: Arise, O Lord, into Thy rest, Thou and the ark of Thy holiness.

Stichos: The Lord hath sworn in truth unto David, and He will not annul it.

Communion Verse: The Lord hath sent redemption unto His people.

THE SUNDAY AFTER THE NATIVITY OF CHRIST: JOSEPH THE BETROTHED, HOLY PROPHET KING DAVID, AND ST. JAMES THE LORD'S BROTHER.

Troparion, Second Tone: O Joseph, proclaim the wonders to David the father of our Divine Lord. Thou hast seen a Virgin conceive; thou hast given glory with the shepherds; thou hast worshipped with the Magi;

and thou hast been warned by an angel. Implore Christ our God to save our souls.

Kontakion, Third Tone: Today divine David is filled with gladness, and together with James, Joseph doth offer praise; for they rejoice at receiving a crown as kinsmen of Christ, and they praise Him Who is ineffably born on earth and they cry: O Compassionate One, save them that honour Thee.

Prokeimenon of the Tone, then of the Saints, Fourth Tone: Wondrous is God in His saints, the God of Israel.

Stichos: In congregations bless ye God, the Lord from the well-springs of Israel.

Alleluia, Fourth Tone: Remember, O Lord, David and all his meekness.

Communion Verse: Praise the Lord from the heavens.... **Another:** Rejoice in the Lord, O ye righteous; praise is meet for the upright.

1 JANUARY: THE CIRCUMCISION OF OUR LORD JESUS CHRIST; ST. BASIL THE GREAT.

Troparion of the Circumcision, First Tone: Thou Who sittest with the Eternal Father on a fiery throne in the heights, wast pleased through the Divine Spirit to be born on earth of a Virgin Maiden, Thy Mother, O Jesus. Wherefore, Thou wast circumcised as a man on the eighth day. Glory to Thine all-gracious will. Glory to Thy providence. Glory to Thy condescension, O only Lover of mankind.

Troparion to St. Basil the Great, First Tone:

Thy fame hath gone forth into all the earth, which hath receive thy word. Thereby thou hast divinely taught the Faith; thou hast made manifest the nature of created things; thou hast made the moral life of men a royal priesthood. O Basil, our righteous father, intercede with Christ God that our souls be saved.

Glory. Kontakion to St. Basil, Fourth Tone:

Thou didst prove to be an unshakable foundation of the church, giving to all mortals an inviolate lordship, and sealing it with thy doctrines O righteous Basil, revealer of heavenly things.

Both now. Kontakion of the Circumcision, Third Tone:

The Lord of all undergoeth circumcision, and in His goodness hath circumcised the sins of mortals. On this day, He giveth the world salvation. And Basil, the hierarch, the Creator's light-bearer and Christ's divine mystic, rejoiceth in the highest.

Prokeimenon Sixth Tone: Save, O Lord, Thy people and bless Thine inheritance.

Stichos: Unto Thee, O Lord, will I cry; O my God, be not silent unto me.

And for St. Basil, First Tone: My mouth shall speak wisdom, and the meditation of my heart shall be of understanding.

Alleluia, Eighth Tone: O Shepherd of Israel attend, Thou that leadest Joseph like a sheep.

Stichos: The mouth of the righteous shall meditate wisdom and his tongue shall speak of judgment.

The Liturgy of Basil the Great is served, and instead of It is truly meet, *we chant* In thee rejoiceth....

Communion Verse: Praise the Lord from the heavens....**Another:** In everlasting remembrance shall the righteous be; he shall not be afraid of evil tidings.

2 JANUARY: THE FOREFEAST OF THEOPHANY and ST. SERAPHIM OF SAROV.

Troparion of the Forefeast, Fourth Tone:

Make ready, O Zabulon,* and prepare thyself, O Nephthalim.* O River Jordan, stand* and leap for joy at receiving the Lord Who cometh to be baptized.* Rejoice, O Adam, with our first mother;* hide not yourselves as in paradise of old.* For seeing us naked, He hath appeared,* that He may clothe us with our first garment.* Christ hath appeared, wishing to renew the whole of creation.

Troparion to St. Seraphim, Fourth Tone:

From thy youth thou didst love Christ, O blessed one, and ardently desiring to work for Him alone thou didst struggle in the wilderness with constant prayer and labour; and having acquired love for Christ with compunction of heart, thou didst prove to be the beloved favorite of the Mother of God. Wherefore, we cry to thee: Save us by thy prayers, O Seraphim, our holy father.

Glory. Kontakion to St. Seraphim, Second Tone: Having left the beauty of the world and what is corrupt in it, O Saint, thou didst settle in Sarov Monastery. And having lived there an angelic life, thou wast for many the way of salvation. Wherefore, Christ hath glorified thee, O Father Seraphim, and hath enriched thee with the gift of healing and miracles. And so we cry to thee: Rejoice, O Seraphim, our holy father.

Both now. Kontakion of the Forefeast, Fourth Tone:

In the running waters of Jordan today the Lord cried to John: Be not afraid to baptize Me, for I am come to save Adam, the first-fashioned man.

Prokeimenon, Alleluia, and Communion Verse for St. Seraphim, same as for St. Job, October 28, page 212.

THE SUNDAY BEFORE HOLY THEOPHANY.

Prokeimenon, Sixth Tone: Save, O Lord, Thy people and bless Thine inheritance.

Stichos: Unto Thee, O Lord, will I cry; O my God, be not, silent unto me.

Alleluia, Eighth Tone: God be gracious unto us and bless us, and cause Thy face to shine upon us.

Communion Verse: Praise the Lord from the heavens, praise Him in the highest.

5 JANUARY: THE EVE OF HOLY THEO-PHANY.

Troparion for the Eve of Theophany, Fourth Tone: The River Jordan was once turned back by the mantle of Elisseus when Elias had been taken up, and the waters were divided hither and thither. And for him the watery path became dry, verily as a type of baptism, whereby we cross the flowing stream of life. Christ hath appeared in the Jordan to sanctify the waters.

Kontakion for the Eve, Fourth Tone: In the running waters of Jordan today the Lord cried to John: Be not afraid to baptize Me, for I am come to save Adam, the first-fashioned man.

Prokeimenon, Third Tone: The Lord is my light and my saviour; whom then shall I fear?

Stichos: The Lord is the defender of my life; of whom then shall I be afraid?

Alleluia, Sixth Tone: My heart hath

poured forth a good word, I speak of my works to the king.

Stichos: Comely art Thou in beauty more than the sons of men.

Communion Verse: Praise the Lord from the heavens....

AT THE GREAT BLESSING OF THE WATERS: Prokeimenon, Third Tone: The Lord is my light and my Saviour; whom then shall I fear?

Stichos: The Lord is the defender of My life; of whom then shall I be afraid?

Alleluia, Fourth Tone: The voice of the Lord is upon the waters; the God of glory hath thundered, the Lord is upon the many waters.

6 JANUARY: THE HOLY THEOPHANY OF OUR LORD GOD AND SAVIOUR JESUS CHRIST.

THE FIRST ANTIPHON, Psalm 113, Second Tone:

Stichos 1: When Israel went out of Egypt, and the house of Jacob from among a barbarous people.

Refrain: Through the prayers of the Theotokos, O Saviour, save us.

Stichos 2: Judea became His sanctuary, Israel His dominion. *Refrain.*

Stichos 3: The sea beheld and fled, Jordan turned back. *Refrain.*

Stichos 4: What aileth thee, O sea, that thou fleddest? And thou Jordan, that thou didst turn back? Refrain.

Glory to the Father, and to the Son, and to the Holy Spirit, both now and ever, and unto the ages of ages. Amen. *Refrain.*

THE SECOND ANTIPHON, Psalm 114, Second Tone:

Stichos 1: I am filled with love, for the Lord will hear the voice of my supplication.

Refrain: O Son of God Who wast baptized in the Jordan, save us who chant unto Thee: Alleluia.

Stichos 2: For He hath inclined His ear unto me, and in my days will I call upon Him. *Refrain.*

Stichos 3: The pangs of death have encompassed me, the perils of hades have found me. Tribulation and sorrow have I found, and I called upon the name of the Lord. *Refrain.*

Stichos 4: Merciful is the Lord and righteous, and our God hath mercy. *Refrain.*

Glory to the Father, and to the Son, and to the Holy Spirit, both now and ever, and unto the ages of ages. Amen.

O Only-begotten Son and Word of God, Who art immortal....

THE THIRD ANTIPHON, Psalm 117, First Tone:

Stichos 1 *(Reader):* O give thanks unto the Lord, for He is good, for His mercy endureth for ever.

CHOIR, **Troparion of the Feast, First Tone:**

When Thou wast baptized in the Jordan, O Lord,* the worship of the Trinity was made manifest;* for the voice of the Father bare witness to Thee,* calling Thee His beloved Son.* And the Spirit in the form of a dove* confirmed the certainty of the word.* O Christ our God, Who hast appeared* and hast enlightened the world, glory be to Thee.

Stichos 2: Let the house of Israel now say that He is good, for His mercy endureth for ever. *Troparion.*

Stichos 3: Let the house of Aaron now say that He is good, for His mercy endureth for ever. *Troparion.*

Stichos 4: Let all that fear the Lord now say that He is good, for His mercy endureth for ever. *Troparion.*

At the Small Entry, the Verse (said by the deacon/priest): Blessed is He that cometh in the name of the Lord. We have blessed you out of the house of the Lord. God is the Lord, and hath appeared unto us.

CHOIR: When Thou wast baptized in the Jordan.... *(See preceding page)*

Glory. Both now. Kontakion, Fourth Tone: Thou hast appeared today unto the whole world,* and Thy light, O Lord, hath been signed upon us* who with knowledge chant unto Thee:* Thou hast come, Thou hast appeared,* O Light Unapproachable.

Instead of the Trisagion: As many as have been baptized into Christ have put on Christ. Alleluia. *Thrice.*

Glory to the Father, and to the Son, and to the Holy Spirit, both now and ever, and unto the ages of ages. Amen. Have put on Christ. Alleluia.

As many as have been baptized into Christ

have put on Christ. Alleluia.

Prokeimenon, Fourth Tone: Blessed is he that cometh in the name of the Lord. God is the Lord, and hath appeared unto us.

Stichos: O give thanks unto the Lord, for He is good, for His mercy endureth for ever.

Alleluia, Fourth Tone: Bring unto the Lord, ye sons of God, bring unto the Lord the sons of rams.

Stichos: The voice of the Lord is upon the waters; the God of glory hath thundered, the Lord is upon the many waters.

Instead of It is truly meet, *we chant the Eirmos of the 9th Ode of the first canon of the feast, Second Tone:*

Refrain: Magnify, O my soul, her who is more honourable than the hosts on high, the most pure Virgin Theotokos.

Eirmos: Every tongue is at a loss to praise thee worthily: even a spirit from the world above is amazed when it seeketh to hymn thee, O Theotokos. But since thou art good, accept our faith: thou knowest well our love inspired by God, for thou art the Protectress of Christians, and thee do we magnify.

Communion Verse: The grace of God that bringeth salvation unto all men hath appeared. *(Titus 2:11)*

22-28 JANUARY: THE SUNDAY OF THE HOLY NEW-MARTYRS AND CONFESSORS Of RUSSIA.

Troparion, Fourth Tone: O ye holy hierarchs, royal passion-bearers and pastors, monks and laymen, men, woman and children, ye countless new-martyrs, confessors, blossoms of the spiritual meadow of Russia, who have borne fruit for Christ in your endurance: Entreat Him, as the One that planted you, that He deliver His people from godless and evil men, and that the Church of Russia be made steadfast through your blood and suffering, unto the salvation of our souls.

Kontakion, Second Tone: O ye new passion-bearers of Russia, who have with your confession finished the course of this earth, receiving boldness through your sufferings: Beseech Christ Who suffered for you, that they who pray to you in the hour of the testing of their faith may receive the gift of courage. For ye are a witness to us who kiss your feet, that neither tribulation, prison, nor death can separate us from the love of God.

Prokeimenon, Fourth Tone: For Thy sake, O Lord, we are slain all the day long *(Ps. 43:20)*

Stichos: We are counted as sheep for the slaughter.

Alleluia. Fourth Tone: The righteous cried, and the Lord heard them, and He delivered them out of all their tribulations.

Communion Verse: Praise the Lord from the heavens.... **And for the New Martyrs:** Rejoice in the Lord, O ye righteous; praise is meet for the upright.

24 JANUARY: BLESSED XENIA, FOOL FOR CHRIST.

Troparion, Fourth Tone: Having renounced the vanity of the earthly world, thou didst take up the cross of a homeless life of wandering; thou didst not fear grief, privation, and the mockery of men, and didst know the love of Christ. Now taking sweet delight of this love in heaven, O Xenia the blessed and divinely wise, pray for the salvation of our souls.

Kontakion, Third Tone: Having been as a wandering stranger on earth, sighing for the heavenly homeland, thou wast known as a fool by the senseless and unbelieving, but as most wise and holy by the faithful, and wast crowned by God with glory and honor, O Xenia, manly-minded and divinely wise. Wherefore, we cry to thee: Rejoice, for after earthly wandering thou hast come to dwell in the Father's house.

Prokeimenon, Fourth Tone: Wondrous is God in His saints, the God of Israel

Stichos: In congregations bless ye God, the Lord from the well-springs of Israel.

Alleluia, First Tone: With patience I waited patiently for the Lord, and He was attentive unto me, and He hearkened unto my supplication.

Stichos: He set my feet upon a rock, and He ordered my steps aright.

Communion Verse: In everlasting remembrance shall the righteous be; he shall not be afraid of evil tidings.

30 JANUARY: THE THREE HIERARCHS: BASIL THE GREAT, GREGORY THE THEOLOGIAN AND JOHN CHRYSOSTOM.

Troparion, First Tone: Let all who love their words come together and honour with hymns the three great luminaries of the Three-sun Godhead: Basil the Great, Gregory the Theologian, and renowned John of golden speech, who have enlightened the world with the rays of their divine doctrines, and are mellifluous rivers of wisdom who have watered all creation with streams of divine knowledge; for they ever intercede with the Trinity for us.

Kontakion, Second Tone: Thou hast taken to Thyself Thy sacred and divinely inspired heralds, the crown of Thy teachers, O Lord, for the enjoyment of Thy blessings and for repose. For Thou hast accepted their sufferings and labours above every whole-burnt offering. O Thou Who alone dost glorify Thy saints.

Prokeimenon, Eighth Tone: Their sound hath gone forth into all the earth, and their words unto the ends of the world.

Stichos: The heavens declare the glory of God, and the firmament proclaimeth the work of His hands.

Alleluia, Fourth Tone: The heavens shall confess Thy wonders, O Lord, and Thy truth in the congregation of saints.

Stichos: God Who is glorified in the council of the saints.

Communion Verse: Rejoice in the Lord, O ye righteous; praise is meet for the upright.

2 FEBRUARY: THE MEETING OF OUR LORD GOD AND SAVIOUR JESUS CHRIST.

At the Small Entry, the Verse (said by the deacon/priest): The Lord hath made known His salvation, in the sight of the nations hath He revealed His righteousness. *(Ps. 97:3)*

CHOIR, **Troparion, First Tone:**

Rejoice, thou who art full of grace, O Virgin Theotokos,* for from thee hath risen the Sun of Righteousness, Christ our God,* enlightening those in darkness.* Rejoice, thou also, O righteous Elder,* as thou receivest in thine arms the Redeemer of our souls,* Who also granteth unto us the Resurrection.

Glory. Both now. Kontakion, First Tone:

Thou Who didst sanctify the Virgin's womb by Thy birth,* and didst bless Symeon's hands as was meet,* by anticipation didst even now save us, O Christ God.* But grant peace in the midst of wars unto Thy commonwealth,* and strengthen Orthodox Christians* whom Thou hast loved, O only Lover of mankind.

Prokeimenon, Third Tone, the Song of the Theotokos: My soul doth magnify the Lord, and my spirit hath rejoiced in God my Saviour.

Stichos: For He hath looked upon the lowliness of His handmaiden; for behold, from henceforth all generations shall call me blessed.

Alleluia, Eighth Tone: Now lettest Thou Thy servant depart in peace, O Master, according to Thy word.

Stichos: A light of revelation for the Gentiles, and the glory of Thy people Israel.

Instead of It is truly meet, *we chant the Eirmos of the 9th Ode of the canon of the feast, Third Tone:*

Refrain: O Virgin Theotokos, thou hope of Christians: Do thou protect, preserve, and save those that hope in thee.

Eirmos: In the law, in the shadow, and the Scriptures, we faithful see a prototype: every male child that first openeth the womb shall be holy unto God; wherefore, the firstborn Word and Son of the Father without beginning, the firstborn Child of a Mother who had not known man, do we magnify.

Communion Verse: I will take the cup of salvation, and I will call upon the name of the Lord.

25 MARCH: THE ANNUNCIATION OF OUR MOST HOLY LADY, THE THEOTOKOS AND EVER-VIRGIN MARY.

Troparion of the Feast, Fourth Tone:

Today is the fountainhead of our salvation* and the manifestation of the mystery which was from eternity.* The Son of God becometh the Virgin's Son,* and Gabriel proclaimeth the good tidings of grace;* wherefore, we also cry to the Theotokos with him:* Rejoice, thou who art full of grace,* the Lord is with thee.

Kontakion, Eighth Tone:

To thee, the champion leader, we thy servants dedicate a feast of victory and of thanksgiving* as ones rescued out of sufferings, O Theotokos;* but as thou art one with might which is invincible,* from all dangers that can be do thou deliver us, that we may cry to thee:* Rejoice, thou Bride Unwedded.

Prokeimenon, Fourth Tone: Proclaim from day to day the good tidings of the salvation of our God. *(Ps. 95:2)*

Stichos: O sing unto the Lord a new song, sing unto the Lord all the earth. *(Ps. 95:1)*

Alleluia, First Tone: He shall come down like rain upon a fleece, and like raindrops that fall upon the earth. *(Ps. 71:6)*

Stichos: His name shall be blessed unto the ages, before the sun doth His name continue.

Instead of It is truly meet, *we chant the Eirmos of the 9th Ode of the canon of the feast, Fourth Tone:*

Refrain: Proclaim, O earth, good tidings of great joy; ye heavens, praise the glory of God.

Eirmos: Let no profane hand touch the living Ark of God, but let the lips of the faithful, chanting unceasingly the words of the angel to the Theotokos, with joy cry out: Rejoice, thou who art full of grace; the Lord is with thee.

Communion Verse: The Lord hath elected Sion, He hath chosen her to be a habitation for Himself. *(Ps. 131:14)*

23 APRIL: THE HOLY GREAT-MARTYR GEORGE THE TROPHY-BEARER.

Troparion, Fourth Tone: As a liberator of captives, defender of the poor, physician of the sick, and champion of kings, O trophy-bearer Great-martyr George, intercede with

Christ God that our souls be saved.

Kontakion, Fourth Tone: Cultivated by God, thou hast proved to be a most honoured cultivator of piety, and thou hast gathered for thyself sheaves of virtues; for having sown in tears, thou reapest in joy, and having suffered with blood, thou hast received Christ. And by thine intercessions, O Saint George, thou grantest unto all forgiveness of sins.

Prokeimenon, Seventh Tone: The righteous man shall be glad in the Lord, and shall hope in Him.

Stichos: Hearken, O God, unto my prayer, when I make supplication unto Thee.

Alleluia, Fourth Tone: The righteous man shall flourish like a palm tree, and like a cedar in Lebanon shall he be multiplied.

Stichos: They that are planted in the house of the Lord, in the courts of our God they shall blossom forth.

Communion Verse: In everlasting remembrance shall the righteous be, he shall not be afraid of evil tidings.

11 MAY: SAINTS CYRIL AND METHODIUS, TEACHERS OF THE SLAVS.

Troparion, Fourth Tone: As ones equal in character to the Apostles and as Teachers of the Slavic lands, O divinely-wise Cyril and Methodius, pray to the Lord of all, to strengten all nations in Orthodoxy and unity of thought, to convert and reconcile the world to God, and to save our souls.

Kontakion, Third Tone: Let us honour our sacred pair of enlightners, who, by translating the divine writings, have poured forth for us a well-spring of divine knowledge from which we draw abundantly even unto this day: We call you blessed, O Cyril and Methodius, ye who stand before the throne of the Most High and intercede fervently for our souls.

Prokeimenon, Seventh Tone: Precious in the sight of the Lord is the death of His saints.

Stichos: What shall I render unto the Lord for all that He hath rendered unto me?

Alleluia, Second Tone: Thy priests shall be clothed with righteousness and Thy righteous shall, rejoice.

Communion Verse: In everlasting remembrance shall the righteous be; he shall not be afraid of evil tidings.

19 JUNE: ST. JOHN THE WONDER-WORKER OF SHANGHAI AND SAN FRANCISCO.

Commemorated on Saturday nearest June 19.

Troparion, Fifth Tone: Thy care for thy flock in its journeyings,* this is a prototype of thy prayers which thou dost ever raise up for all the world;* thus we believe, having known thy love, O holy Hierarch and Wonderworker John.* Entirely sanctified by God through the sacred ministry of the Holy Mysteries,* and being thereby ever strengthened,* thou didst hasten to those who suffer, O most gladsome healer.* Hasten now also to the help of us who with all our heart honour thee.

Kontakion, Fourth Tone: Thy heart is open wide for all,* who entreat thee with love, O holy Hierarch John,* and who remember the ascetical struggles of thy labourious life,* and thy painless and gentle repose,* O faithful servant of the most pure Directress.

At Matins and Molebens, **Prokeimenon, Fourth Tone:** Precious in the sight of the Lord is the death of His saints.

Stichos: What shall I render unto the Lord

for all that He hath rendered unto me?

For Liturgy, see St. Nicholas, page 219.

23 JUNE: THE MEETING OF THE WONDER-WORKING ICON OF OUR LADY OF VLADIMIR.

Troparion, Fourth Tone: Today the most glorious city of Moscow rejoiceth radiantly,* for it receiveth as a ray of the sun thy wonder-working icon, O Lady;* and as we now have recourse to it, we pray to thee and cry:* O most wonderful Lady Theotokos,* pray to Christ our God, Who was incarnate of thee,* that this city and all Christian cities and countries* may be kept unharmed from all assaults of the enemy,* and that our souls be saved,* for He is merciful.

Kontakion, Eighth Tone: O Champion leader, defender of our souls,* we joyfully celebrate the festival of thy meeting, O our Lady Theotokos;* for thou hast delivered us from evils by the coming of thy precious icon,* and as is meet we cry unto thee:* Rejoice, O Bride Unwedded.

Prokeimenon, Alleluia, and Communion Verse – same as for November 21 (page 216).

24 JUNE: THE NATIVITY OF THE HOLY AND GLORIOUS PROPHET, FORERUNNER, AND BAPTIST JOHN.

Troparion, Fourth Tone: O Prophet and Forerunner of the coming of Christ,* we who honour thee with love are unable to extol thee worthily;* for by thy holy and august birth* the barrenness of thy mother and the speechlessness of thy father were loosened,* and the incarnation of the Son of God is proclaimed to the world.

Kontakion, Third Tone: She that was formerly barren giveth birth today to the Forerunner of Christ,* Who is the fulfillment of all prophecy;* for He Whom the prophets foretold is God the Word* Who hath appeared to the prophet, herald, and forerunner* when he laid his hand on Him in the Jordan.

Prokeimenon, Seventh Tone: The righteous man shall be glad in the Lord, and shall hope in Him.

Stichos: Hearken, O God, unto my prayer, when I make supplication unto Thee.

Alleluia, First Tone: Blessed be the Lord God of Israel, for He hath visited and wrought redemption for His people.

Stichos: And thou, O Child, shalt be called the prophet of the Most High.

Communion Verse: In everlasting remembrance shall the righteous be; he shall not be afraid of evil tidings.

29 JUNE: THE HOLY FIRST LEADERS OF THE APOSTLES, PETER AND PAUL.

Troparion, Fourth Tone: O foremost of the Apostles* and teachers of the world,* intercede with the Master of all,* that He grant peace to the world* and to our souls great mercy.

Kontakion, Second Tone: Thou hast taken to Thyself, O Lord,* the firm and divine-voiced preachers, the chief Apostles,* for the enjoyment of Thy blessings and for repose;* for Thou didst accept their labours and death as above all sacrifice,* O Thou Who alone knowest the secrets of our hearts.

Prokeimenon, Eighth Tone: Their sound hath gone forth into all the earth, and their words unto the ends of the world.

Stichos: The heavens declare the glory of God, and the firmament proclaimeth the work of His hands.

Alleluia, First Tone: The heavens shall confess Thy wonders, O Lord.

Stichos: God Who is glorified in the council of the saints.

Communion Verse: Their sound hath gone forth into all the earth, and their words unto the ends of the world.

4 JULY: THE HOLY PASSION-BEARERS: TSAR-MARTYR NICHOLAS, TSARITSA-MARTYR ALEXANDRA, MARTYRED CROWN-PRINCE ALEXIS, THE ROYAL MARTYRS OLGA, TATIANA, MARIA, AND ANASTASIA; AND THE HOLY NUN-MARTYRS, GRAND DUCHESS ELIZABETH AND NUN BARBARA.

Troparion, Fifth Tone: Meekly didst thou endure bonds and divers sufferings,* and the loss of an earthly kingdom,* and didst bear witness for Christ even unto death (at the hands of) those that fight against God,* O great passion-bearer, divinely-crowned Tsar Nicholas;* therefore, Christ God hath crowned thee in the heavens with a martyr's crown,* together with thy queen, thy children, and thy servants.* Him do thou entreat to have mercy on the Russian land and save our souls.

Kontakion, Sixth Tone: Hope made strong the Tsar-martyr with his queen and children and servants,* and incited them ardently toward Thy love,* thereby foreshadowing for them the future rest;* through their intercessions, O Lord, have mercy on us.

Prokeimenon, Fourth Tone: For Thy sake, O Lord, we are slain all the day long.

Stichos: We are counted as sheep for the slaughter.

Alleluia, First Tone: Our God is refuge and strength, a helper in afflictions which mightily befall us.

Stichos: O Lord, save the king, and hearken unto us in the day when we call upon Thee.

Communion Verse: Be glad in the Lord, O ye righteous; praise is meet for the upright.

5 JULY: THE UNCOVERING OF THE RELICS OF ST. SERGIUS OF RADONEZH.

Troparion, Eighth Tone: Thou didst receive Christ in thy soul from thy youth, O Saint,* and above all didst desire to be quit of the turmoil of the world.* Thou didst courageously settle in the wilds,* and there thou didst raise children of obedience, fruits of humility.* Thus as an abode of the Trinity, thou didst enlighten with thy miracles all who came to thee with faith,* and didst grant healings abundantly to all.* O our Father Sergius, pray to Christ our God that He save our souls.

Kontakion, Eighth Tone: Having risen from the earth, thou didst shine today like the sun;* for thy precious and incorrupt relics were found like a fragrant flower,* shining with a multitude of miracles and pouring various healings on all the faithful,* and gladdening thy chosen flock, which thou didst gather so wisely and tend so well.* And now as thou standest in the presence of the Trinity,* pray for them and for all Orthodox Christians, that we may cry to thee:* Rejoice, O divinely-wise Sergius.

Prokeimenon, Alleluia, and Communion Verse — same as for St. Job of Pochaev, October 28, page 212.

15 JULY: GREAT PRINCE AND EQUAL-OF-THE-APOSTLES SAINT VLADIMIR.

Troparion, Fourth Tone: Thou wast like a

merchant that seeketh a beautiful pearl, O glorious sovereign Vladimir,* sitting on the height of the throne of the mother of cities, God-protected Kiev.* Searching and sending to the imperial city to know the Orthodox Faith,* thou didst find Christ, the priceless Pearl,* Who chose thee as a second Paul,* and Who did shake off thy spiritual and physical blindness in the holy font.* Wherefore, we who are thy people celebrate thy falling asleep.* Pray that thy Russian land be saved,* and that Orthodox people be granted peace and great mercy.

Kontakion, Eighth Tone: Like the great Apostle Paul, O most glorious Vladimir,* in old age thou didst leave off all zeal for idols as a childish sophism,* and as a full-grown man thou wast adorned with the royal purple of divine baptism.* And now as thou standest in joy in the presence of Christ the Saviour,* pray that thy Russian land be saved,* and that Orthodox people be granted peace and great mercy.

Prokeimenon, Third Tone: O chant unto our God, chant ye; chant unto our King, chant ye.

Stichos: Clap your hands, all ye nations; shout unto God with a voice of rejoicing.

Alleluia, Sixth Tone: I have raised up one chosen out of My people.

Stichos: For My hand shall be unto him an ally, and Mine arm shall strengthen him. *(Ps.88)*

Communion Verse: In everlasting remembrance shall the righteous be; he shall not be afraid of evil tidings.

16 JULY: COMMEMORATION OF THE HOLY FATHERS OF THE FIRST SIX ECUMENICAL COUNCILS.

If this date fall on Wednesday or earlier, they are commemorated on the preceding Sunday. If on Thursday or later, then on the following Sunday.

Troparion of the Resurrection, and of the Holy Fathers, Eighth Tone: Most Glorified art Thou, O Christ our God,* Who hast established our holy fathers as luminous stars upon the earth,* and through them didst guide us all to the true Faith.* O Most-merciful One, glory be to Thee.

Kontakion of the Resurrection. Glory. **Of the Fathers, Eighth Tone:**

The preaching of the apostles and the doctrines of the fathers confirmed the one Faith of the Church.* And wearing the garment of truth woven from the theology on high,* She rightly divideth and glorifieth the great mystery of piety.

Both now. *Kontakion of the temple or* O Protection of Christians....

Prokeimenon of the Tone, then the Song of the Fathers, Fourth Tone: Blessed art Thou, O Lord, the God of our fathers, and praised and glorified is Thy name unto the ages.

Alleluia of the Tone, and of the Fathers, First Tone: The God of gods, the Lord, hath spoken, and He hath called the earth from the rising of the sun, and unto the setting thereof.

Stichos: Gather together unto Him His holy ones who have established His covenant upon sacrifices.

Communion Verse: Praise the Lord from the heavens....**And:** Rejoice in the Lord, O ye righteous; praise is meet for the upright.

19 JULY: THE UNCOVERING OF THE RELICS OF ST. SERAPHIM.

Troparion and Kontakion same as January 2,

page 235. Prokeimenon, and Communion Verse same as for St. Job, October 28, page 212.

20 JULY: THE HOLY AND GLORIOUS PROPHET ELIAS.

Troparion, Fourth Tone: The incarnate angel, the summit of the prophets,* the forerunner of the coming of Christ,* Elias the glorious from on high did send down grace to Elisseus;* he driveth away diseases and cleanseth lepers.* Wherefore, he poureth forth healings upon them that honor him.

Kontakion, Second Tone: O renowned Elias, prophet and seer of the mighty works of God,* who by thy word didst check the torrential rain-clouds:* pray for us to the only Lover of mankind.

Prokeimenon Fourth Tone: Thou art a priest for ever, after the order of Melchisedek.

Stichos: The Lord said unto my Lord: Sit Thou at My right and, until I make Thine enemies the footstool of Thy feet.

Alleluia, Fourth Tone: Moses and Aaron among His priests, and Samuel among them that call upon His name.

Communion Verse: In everlasting remembrance shall the righteous be; he shall not be afraid of evil tidings.

27 JULY: THE GREAT-MARTYR AND HEALER ST. PANTELEIMON.

Troparion, Third Tone: O holy passion-bearer and healer Panteleimon,* intercede with the merciful God* that He grant unto our souls* forgiveness of offences.

Kontakion, Fifth Tone: As an imitator of the Merciful One,* and as one who received from Him the grace of healing,* O passion-bearer and martyr of Christ our God,* by thy prayers heal the diseases of our souls,* and ever banish the snares of the enemy from them that cry with faith:* Save us, O Lord.

Prokeimenon, Fourth Tone: Wondrous is God in His saints, the God of Israel.

Stichos: In congregations bless ye God, the Lord from the well-springs of Israel.

Alleluia, Second Tone: The righteous man shall flourish like a palm tree, and like a cedar in Lebanon shall he be multiplied.

Communion Verse: In everlasting remembrance shall the righteous be; he shall not be afraid of evil tidings.

1 AUGUST: THE PROCESSION OF THE VENERABLE WOOD OF THE PRECIOUS AND LIFE-GIVING CROSS.

And the Commemoration of the Holy Seven Maccabee Children, their mother Solomonia, and their teacher Eleazar.

Troparion to the Precious Cross, First Tone: Save, O Lord, Thy people* and bless Thine inheritance;* grant Thou unto Orthodox Christians victory over enemies;* and by the power of Thy Cross do Thou preserve Thy commonwealth.

Troparion to the Holy Maccabees, First Tone: The sufferings of the saints,* which they suffered for thee, be, O Lord, a supplication,* and heal all our diseases,* O Lover of mankind, we pray.

Kontakion to the Cross, Fourth Tone: O Thou Who wast lifted up willingly on the Cross,* bestow Thy mercies upon the new community named after Thee, O Christ God;* gladden with Thy power the Orthodox Christians,* granting them victory over enemies;* may they have as Thy help the weapon of peace, the invincible trophy.

Kontakion to the Holy Maccabees, Second Tone: O seven pillars of the wisdom of God,* and seven-branched candlestick of the Divine Light,* ye were great martyrs before the martyrs, O supremely-wise Maccabees.* With them pray to the God of all* that they who venerate you may be saved.

Prokeimenon to the Cross, Sixth Tone: Save, O Lord, Thy people and bless Thine inheritance.

Stichos: Unto Thee, O Lord, will I cry; O my God, be not silent unto me.

And the Prokeimenon for the Maccabees, Fourth Tone: In the saints that are in His earth hath the Lord been wondrous; He hath wrought all His desires in them.

Alleluia, First Tone: Remember Thy congregation which Thou hast purchased from the beginning.

Stichos: But God is our king before the ages, He hath wrought salvation in the midst of the earth.

And for the Maccabees, Fourth Tone: The righteous cried, and the Lord heard them, and He delivered them out of all their tribulations.

Communion Verse to the Cross: The light of Thy countenance, O Lord, hath been signed upon us.

And for the Maccabees: Rejoice in the Lord, O ye righteous; praise is meet for the upright.

6 AUGUST: THE HOLY TRANSFIGURATION OF OUR LORD GOD AND SAVIOUR JESUS CHRIST.

The First Antiphon, Psalm 65, Second Tone:

Stichos 1: Shout with jubilation unto the Lord all the earth;* chant ye unto His name, give glory in praise of Him.

Refrain: Through the prayers of the Theotokos, O Saviour, save us.

Stichos 2: The voice of Thy thunder is in their rolling.* And Thy lightnings have lightened the world; the earth was shaken and it trembled. *Refrain.*

Stichos 3: Confession and majesty hast Thou put on,* Who coverest Thyself with light as with a garment. *Refrain.*

Glory to the Father, and to the Son, and to the Holy Spirit,* both now and ever, and unto the ages of ages. Amen. *Refrain.*

The Second Antiphon, Psalm 47, Second Tone:

Stichos 1: The mountains of Sion on the sides of the north,* the city of the great King.

Refrain: O Son of God Who wast transfigured upon the mountain, save us who chant unto Thee: Alleluia.

Stichos 2: And He brought them unto the mountain of His sanctuary,* this mountain which His right hand had gained as a possession. *Refrain.*

Stichos 3: Mount Sion which He loved,* and He built His sanctuary like that of a unicorn. *Refrain.*

Glory to the Father, and to the Son, and to the Holy Spirit, both now and ever, and unto the ages of ages. Amen.

O Only-begotten Son and Word of God, Who art immortal....

The Third Antiphon, Psalm 124:

Stichos 1 *(Reader):* They that trust in the Lord shall be as Mount Sion; nevermore shall they be shaken.

CHOIR, **Troparion, Seventh Tone:**

Thou wast transfigured on the mountain, O Christ our God,* showing to Thy disciples Thy glory as each one could endure;* shine forth Thou on us, who are sinners all, Thy light ever-unending* through the prayers of the Theotokos. O Light-giver, glory to Thee.

Stichos 2: Mountains are round about her, and the Lord is round about His people from henceforth and for evermore. *Troparion.*

Stichos 3: O Lord, who shall abide in Thy tabernacle? and who shall dwell in Thy holy mountain? *Troparion.*

Stichos 4: Who shall ascend into the mountain of the Lord? Or who shall stand in His holy place? *Troparion.*

At the Small Entry the Verse (said by the deacon/priest): O Lord, send out Thy light and Thy truth; they have guided me along the way, and have brought me unto Thy holy mountain.

CHOIR: Thou wast transfigured on the mountain... (*see above*).

Glory. Both now. Kontakion, Seventh Tone:

On the mount Thou wast transfigured,* and Thy disciples, as much as they could bear, beheld Thy glory, O Christ God;* so that when they should see Thee crucified,* they would know Thy passion to be willing,* and would preach to the world* that Thou, in truth, art the Effulgence of the Father.

Prokeimenon, Fourth Tone: How magnified are Thy works, O Lord! In wisdom hast Thou made them all.

Stichos: Bless the Lord, O my soul; O Lord my God, Thou hast been magnified exceedingly.

Alleluia, Eighth Tone: Thine are the heavens, and Thine is the earth.

Stichos: Blessed is the people that knoweth jubilation.

Instead of It is truly meet, *we chant the Eirmos of the 9th Ode of the first canon, Fourth Tone:*

Refrain: Magnify, O my soul, the Lord transfigured on Tabor.

Eirmos: Thy birthgiving was shown to be incorrupt:* God came forth from thy womb,* and He appeared on earth wearing flesh* and dwelt among men;* wherefore, O Theotokos, we all magnify thee.

Communion Verse: O Lord, in the light of

Thy face shall we walk, and in Thy name shall we rejoice for ever.

13 AUGUST: ST. TIKHON OF ZADONSK.

On this day also the Apodosis of the Feast of the Transfiguration.

Troparion to St. Tikhon, Eighth Tone:

From thy youth thou didst love Christ, O blessed one,* and thou wast a model to all in word, life, love, spirit,* faith, purity, and humility.* Wherefore, thou hast now taken up thy dwelling in the heavenly mansions* where, as thou standest before the throne of the Most Holy Trinity,* O Saint Tikhon, pray that our souls be saved.

Kontakion, Eighth Tone: O successor of the apostles, adornment of hierarchs,* teacher of the Orthodox Church:* pray to the Lord of all to grant peace to the world,* and to our souls great mercy.

Prokeimenon, Alleluia, and Communion same as for St. Nectarius, November 9, page 214.

15 AUGUST: THE DORMITION OF OUR MOST HOLY LADY, THE THEO-TOKOS AND EVER-VIRGIN MARY.

Troparion, First Tone:

In giving birth thou didst preserve thy virginity;* in thy dormition thou didst not forsake the world, O Theotokos.* Thou wast translated unto life,* since thou art the Mother of Life;* and by thine intercessions dost thou deliver our souls from death.

Glory. Both now. Kontakion, Second Tone:

The grave and death could not hold the Theotokos,* who is sleepless in her intercessions and an unfailing hope in her mediations.* For as the Mother of Life she was translated unto life* by Him Who dwelt in her ever-virgin womb.

Prokeimenon, Third Tone, the Song of the Theotokos: My soul doth magnify the Lord, and my spirit hath rejoiced in God my Saviour.

Stichos: For He hath looked upon the lowliness of His handmaiden; for behold, from henceforth all generations shall call me blessed.

Alleluia, Second Tone: Arise, O Lord, into Thy rest, Thou and the ark of Thy holiness.

Stichos: The Lord hath sworn in truth unto David, and will not annul it.

Instead of It is truly meet, *we chant the Eirmos of the 9th Ode of the first canon of the feast, First*

Tone:

Refrain: The angels, having beheld the Dormition of the Most Pure One,* were struck with wonder,* at how the Virgin went up from earth to heaven.

Eirmos: Overcome in thee are the bounds of nature, O pure Virgin:* for childbirth is virginal, and life is betrothed to death;* virgin after bearing child, and alive after death,* thou dost ever save, O Theotokos, thine inheritance.

Communion Verse: I will take the cup of salvation, and I will call upon the name of the Lord.

16 AUGUST: THE TRANSLATION OF THE HOLY ICON "NOT MADE BY HANDS" OF OUR LORD JESUS CHRIST FROM EDESSA TO CONSTANTINOPLE.

Troparion, Second Tone: We worship Thine immaculate Icon, O Good One,* asking the forgiveness of our failings, O Christ God;* for of Thine own will Thou wast well-pleased to ascend the Cross in the flesh* that Thou mightest deliver from slavery to the enemy those whom Thou hadst fashioned.* Wherefore, we cry to Thee thankfully:* Thou didst fill all things with joy, O our Saviour, when Thou camest to save the world.

Kontakion, Second Tone: The Uncircumscribable Word of the Father* was circumscribed when He took flesh of thee, O Theotokos;* and when He had restored the defiled image to its ancient state,* He suffused it with divine beauty.* As for us, confessing our salvation,* we record it in deed and word.

Prokeimenon, Fourth Tone: O sing unto the Lord a new song, for the Lord hath wrought wondrous things.

Stichos: All the ends of the earth have seen the salvation of our God.

Alleluia Fourth Tone: O Lord, in the light of Thy face shall we walk, and in Thy name shall we rejoice unto the ages. *(Ps. 88:15)*

28 AUGUST: THE UNCOVERING OF THE RELICS OF ST. JOB OF POCHAEV.

Troparion, Kontakion, Prokeimenon, Alleluia, and Communion Verse same as page 211-212.

29 AUGUST: THE BEHEADING OF ST. JOHN THE BAPTIST.

Troparion, Second Tone: The memory of

the righteous is celebrated with hymns of praise,* but the Lord's testimony is sufficient for thee, O Forerunner;* for thou hast proved to be truly even more venerable than the prophets,* since thou wast granted to baptize in the running waters Him Whom they proclaimed.* Wherefore, having contested for the truth, thou didst rejoice to announce the good tidings even to those in hades:* that God hath appeared in the flesh,* taking away the sin of the world and granting us great mercy.

Kontakion, Fifth Tone: The glorious beheading of the Forerunner was a certain Divine dispensation,* that the coming of the Saviour might also be preached to those in hades.* Lament then, Herodias, that thou hast demanded a wicked murder,* for thou didst love neither the law of God nor eternal life,* but one false and fleeting.

Prokeimenon, Seventh Tone: The righteous man shall be glad in the Lord, and shall hope in Him.

Stichos: Hearken, O God, unto my prayer, when I make supplication unto Thee.

Alleluia, Fourth Tone: The righteous man

shall flourish like a palm tree, and like a cedar in Lebanon shall he be multiplied.

Stichos: They that are planted in the house of the Lord, in the courts of our God they shall blossom forth.

Communion Verse: In everlasting remembrance shall the righteous be; he shall not be afraid of evil tidings.

THE END OF THE MENAION

✤✤✤✤✤✤